A Cry of HOPE

Spiritual Reality Therapy

Santiago C. Estrada, Ph.D. Psychology

Published by:
Salsa Books
247 Forest Avenue
Laguna Beach, CA 92651

No part of this book may be
reproduced in any form
without permission
from the publisher.

ISBN 0-916221-00-8

Foreword

The story of the spiritual quest is as old as mankind. It exists in all cultures of all nations of the world. *"A Cry of Hope"* is as moving, revealing, and beautiful as the best of these stories.

I have known Dr. Estrada since he has been sober. He has overcome poverty, prejudice, and tremendous odds. He is a sincere, compassionate, wise, enthusiastic man, who truely cares about his fellows. In finding himself and fulfilling his purpose in life, the writer shares the formula of his success in the struggle of continuous spiritual comprehension. The wise reader will use this formula in the pursuit of his own personal enlightenment.

> *"To know others is wisdom.*
> *To know yourself is enlightenment."*
>
> *Zen Saying*

John A. Newsome, M.D.
Medical Director
GENESIS, Chemical Dependency Program
South Coast Medical Center
South Laguna, California

Dedication

To my family, for their love and honesty,
Kim, Michelle and Gabriel;
and to my parents, for trying their best,
the late Santiago Rodriquez Estrada
and Guadalupe Carreno Estrada.

Acknowledgements

I would like to thank all those persons who have made
this book a reality. In particular, Jim Messelbeck of
Allergan, Inc.; Joseph Wolpe, Ph.D.;
Douglass Chalmer, Ph.D.; and Eric Speare, M.D.
For their prayers and spiritual guidance,
Fr. Charles, Fr. Shepperd, Fr. Robert,
and William L.
For her encouragement and lasting friendship, Sibbers,
For his laughter and acceptance
the late Fr. Dave O. Duran.
For their immeasurable love and reality checks,
Lynn W. and my brother, Victor.

Table of Contents

Introduction

This book is a personal testimony and case study of how hope can be a living catalyst for the chemically and emotionally addicted. Foremost, it is an effort to reach out to the lonely and suffering and to their families or loved ones who also may be suffering. In June of 1976, I began to write my feelings and thoughts concerning my fellow men and women. One introduction stated, "My story is your story. It is complex yet simple, because reality is simply complex." This book has had many titles that have ranged from Contemporary Curanderism (folk psychiatry), Jimmy, Jim, Santiago what next?, to Being Human. That introduction went on to express, "If you are a person who is being or trying to be more human, that is, if you are in the process of life and living life in such a manner that people matter, then I speak to you. Whether you are poor, rich, average, this story is about you because you bleed, cry, scream, struggle, laugh, desire, drink, talk to yourself, want and need others, care for others, and want to be loved. This story is for all *"ser humanos"* - human beings - and those who have a desire to be more human." That was June 1976 and that is how far the book got.

Today is June 27, 1985, and I am writing the last draft of this introduction from Prince of Peace Abbey, A Benedictine monastery, Benet Hill, Oceanside, California. As I compare the draft of 1976 to this draft, my heart is warmed because the intent has not changed in eleven years; the difference is - now there is a manuscript to accompany the introduction. That is a significant difference!

The intent is to reach out to you and to share with you my experience, strength, weakness, and most of all my CRY OF HOPE. This book is the growth from a seed within me that has been encouraged to bloom by the lives of literally thousands of young people, adult men and women, corporate executives, prisoners, and alcoholics and addicts who have touched my professional and personal life by their willingness to allow me to join them in their painful and sometimes joyful search for hope. In 1976, I met Leo Buscaglia, the love teacher, and I was near the end of my journey here on this earth, so I thought. It was our first and last meeting. We were discussing my career choices and completing my dissertation before I left the northwest. Near the end of our conversation, he said something like,

"The only real answer is to immerse yourself in love." As I walked out of his office I thought, "That's impossible for me." So, I introduce you to a personal effort, to add to your life, by writing in the spirit of the greatest dimension of all, love, which is to consider, respect and strive to see the needs of the beloved - which in this case, is you, my human family.

This path of love has become more real to me as hope has become a conscious part of my life. Learning to be still and quiet has increased my belief that I have much more in common with you than I have differences. I believe this sense of "we" rather than "I" has grown because of a miracle or set of miracles that have and continue to impact my life. Although I acknowledge the uniqueness of each person and consider cultural awareness to be essential in human understanding, the major needs of human beings are universal. I believe that we prefer that which enhances life, i.e., peace, honesty, respect, mutual recognition, cooperation, but the reality is that many times we choose the opposite of that which enhances our personal life and lives of others.

I know that there have been many times when I chose to nurture, feed, fan that spark of the less-preferred way until I was consumed in an inferno of feelings, thoughts and actions contrary to my basic preference and basic nature.

I also reach out to families, loved ones and friends who are close or emotionally involved with those persons, who like myself, seemed to be pulled in a powerful vacuum of self-centeredness, obsession, anxiety and hopelessness. I ask you to read and see how you are part of the disease which appears to be the inability to belong, to love and to receive love.

Now, I must tell you that in June of 1976 my life was in turmoil and there was no manuscript because I could not stay focused on anything. I cannot to my satisfaction describe the miracle that has launched my life's journey of devotion, dedication, openness, willingness and faith that there is a real and viable purpose to my presence on this planet Earth. Yet I must say that there are sill moments when fear, guilt, frustration, self-centeredness and alienation will spread like a dark gray cloud over my consciousness and color my behavior and flavor my life. However, these emotions have lost the power to rule an entire day.

It is this new freedom that this book is about, so please join me, by allowing yourself to read the story that is to follow. First, I would like you to use your visual and creative powers by placing yourself in a comfortable, pleasant and safe environment and imagine listening to this story. Secondly, as you read, check the feelings, thoughts or behaviors you identify with. (Please feel free to write me if you have any questions, comments or send your personal story if you wish to share it with me. I will do my best to answer you as soon as possible.) Thirdly, if certain sections are very important, write down the reactions that these sections may elicit immediately. When you have finished reading my story, you may choose to go on and write you own story. Read and follow the suggested program that I call "Spiritual Reality Therapy"(SRT), an approach to counseling and holistic human growth that I have developed over the past sixteen years of being a family therapist, educator and organizational consultant. You will find an brief background to SRT; my definitions of self-esteem, self-worth, self-regard, and self-transformation. How it works, is to start and finish your story; writing your story is a major part of the approach. Coming to believe that there is real hope and living like there is, is the result.

Herman Hesse's words served as an inspiration to me. Perhaps they can help you. They are as follows: "Every man (and woman) is more than just himself; he also represents the unique, the very special and always significant and remarkable point at which the world phenomena intersect, only once in this way and never again. That is why every man's story is important, eternal, sacred; that is why every man, as long as he lives, fulfills the will of nature, is wondrous and worthy of every consideration. In each individual the spirit has become flesh, in each man the creation suffers, within each one a redeemer is nailed to the cross."

CHAPTER 1

Personal Historical Antecedents

Both my father and mother were born in Mexico, a land that I do not know very well, but a culture that is a strong part of my identity. Juchipila is the town where my father was born. It was one of the first areas settled in New Spain. He told me that this land brought forth sugarcane, and it was the sugarcane that sustained his family. Supposedly, my grandfather was a full-blooded Indian and my grandmother was a Mestiza, which is a mixture of Indian and Spanish blood. My father said my grandfather began a small farm by breeding mules and growing a small acreage of sugarcane. My grandmother was very insistent that her children learn to read and write. She was able to persuade my grandfather that for the future of her children, this was absolutely necessary. My father told me it was because of my grandmother he learned to read and write.

My father told me a story that occurred one morning when he was about 19 years old. He and his brother Tomas were tending the mules. All of a sudden in the early dawn they heard the thunder of galloping horses. My father jumped to his feet, looked in the distance and saw the dust rising up in clouds as the horses galloped toward his father's house. His heart began to beat rapidly and his mind raced as he concluded that the horses were probably being ridden by revolutionaries. He mounted a mule and rode as fast as he could toward the house following the dust clouds. When he approached the house, he saw a body hanging between two trees. The body was his father. The revolutionaries had hung him by his wrists and had beaten him to death. My father ran to his father and untied his wrists. He looked at him in absolute helplessness. In his tremendous panic, he suddenly remembered that his mother might also have been hurt. In search of her, he ran into the house. He remembered then that his mother had gone to visit her sister.

I do not know much more about the story, except that since the entire family had been threatened with death from the revolutionaries, the family scattered. My father came to the United States in 1925. I have read the letters that were written to my father from his mother. She begged him not to return to Mexico and assured him that she was safe. She felt that the threat was directed more toward her sons than anyone else. My grandmother died after my father had been in the United States a year. This is all I know of my father's side of the family, for I was never to meet any of them.

My father traveled throughout the United States. He spent a part of his life in Illinois and in Colorado. Finally, he came west to California and settled in a small town called Claremont, where he lived for a few years. He then moved to Fullerton to pick citrus fruit, oranges and lemons. Then, Fullerton had a population of about 7,000 people. It was there that he met my mother in a small restaurant. My father was forty-eight years old and my mother was thirty-four. She was a waitress at this restaurant where my father ate regularly.

My mother was also born in Mexico, in a small town called "Valle de Topia". My mom was not very sure where her dad came from, except that he was a Spaniard. My Aunt Luz relayed the following history. My grandfather was a small man, about five feet tall. He was extremely pale and had green eyes. He was also very business-wise. My grandfather worked until he had enough money to purchase a male and a female goat. With the two goats, he began to make cheese and to breed more goats. As a result of his business instinct, he was able to buy small bits of land which he amassed into a ranch. He married my grandmother, whom he adored. She was of Mexican and Spanish blood. My grandmother had twenty children, four of whom died at birth. My mother was the last of the children who lived. When my mother was eight years old, her mother died. She would cry when she would tell this part of her story. A few months after that, her father died. There were tremendous struggles between her brothers and sisters for the land and for power. As a result of this, my Aunt Luz married her fiance and they took my mother with them to the United States. My aunt and her new husband also brought along his brother. This man and my mother were wed on their way to the United States; my mother was twelve years old. This man was not my father, but was the father of my three sisters and three brothers. My aunt has told me that my mother and her new husband were often close to starvation. They finally made it across the border and lived in Yuma, Arizona for a short while before settling in Anaheim, California.

My mother told me that her life was very difficult during those years. Her young husband was not willing to work regularly. He was a singer and spent much of his time entertaining, but not getting paid. There were arguments and periods of anguish. Six children and a number of years later, her husband committed a crime, which brought great shame to her and to the family. He was taken to jail and tried. The sentence was as follows: He could go to prison for a long period of time, or he could choose to go to Mexico and never return. He chose to go to Mexico and not return. When he left, his last born, my brother Victor, was less than a year old. Mexico and her culture was to impact our lives in varied ways.

The Mexican culture is very rich and diversified; it also is quite complex. I need to express my relationship to it by sharing a poem in the form of a dream. The dream unfolded like this: I was a young boy in the midst of many people who were dressed in bright feathers and they were a small, dark reddish-brown people full of energy and tremendous intensity that touched the depth of my soul. Suddenly I found myself being led by an old man through the mountains and this old man had a face with a thousand wrinkles in it, long white hair and the body of a young warrior. He took me to a stream where the water was clear and I could see his face and mine side by side. He then took some wet sand in his left hand and with his right hand he began to roll it into a small ball which he blew on three times. Then, three beautiful gems fell to the ground. He said, "Gem number one, my son - it has been 4,000 years since our seed was planted here, and now we are at the dawn of a new world. Our god *Quetzalcoatl*, the integration of man and animal, earth and sky, sailed off around the 12th Century on a raft made of serpents and promised to return in one reed (52 years). Gem number two - our cousins, the Aztecs, completed their city Tenochtelan in 1325 and when you awake from this dream, you will read that Cortes, the Spanish conquistador, was thought to be *Quetzalcoatl* because he was white and bearded, rode a horse which made him look like half man and half animal." He went on to say, "There will be many legends and myths about that time; the people and their ways will be divided and the division will be an illusion, just as time is an illusion. Gem number three - a country will grow to be known as Mexico and Mexicans will have Indian and Spanish blood. Part of Mexico will be taken by America; some Mexicans will return to Mexico, others will remain to become part of America. Throughout the years, more and more Mexicans will go north to America. You, my son, will be an American of Mexican descent, a Spanish and English– speaking Indian." Then the old man turned into a young man who said, "I am Huextozin, an Aztec prince of Texcoco and this is what I said to the Spanish at the sunset of our time:

You tell me that I must perish
like the flowers that I cherish.
Nothing remaining of my name,
nothing remembered of my fame?

6

But the gardens I planted still are young,
the songs I sang will still be sung..."

Then I saw my father, the Indian, who took my mother, the Spaniard, by the hand and they began to dance. The old man calmly whispered in my ear, "Remember, my son, there is only one time - no time in the back - no time in the front - just this time - the time to be," and I awoke and I was born.

CHAPTER 2

Orange Nightmares and Midnight Bandits

My story starts with a dream I had at the age of five. In my dream, I was a strong young man. For some odd reason I was dressed in very loud-colored clothes that fit tightly. A man was leading me into a large tent and as we got closer, I could hear the roar of a crowd gathered inside. Next, I was climbing up a long ladder that had many steps. Up to this point I was calm and enjoying the excitement. When I reached the top of the ladder, I noticed there was a fire raging in the center of a ring in which the ladder stood, and my mother was standing in the middle surrounded by flames. A man threw a swing and signaled for me to take it so I could save my mom. Nervous excitement rushed through my entire body. I wanted to save her and at the same time I wanted to run away. Fear permeated my mind; I couldn't run and I couldn't save my mom. I called out for it to be a dream; suddenly, I woke up to my mother's singing. It was a relief to see that I was home, and that both my mother and I were safe.

Our house was in Anaheim, a small town of less than 15,000 people. When I was a child, within the parameters of my world, there were no freeways, no Disneyland, and no large factories. There were orange groves that seemed to stretch for miles around my home. I can remember the smell of orange blossoms and the euphoric intoxication they induced. That fragrance was addicting and I could never get enough of it.

My father was a professional orange picker and he seemed to take pride in what he did. He went to great lengths to prepare his orange clippers, cantina, hat, shoes and his Levi jacket. I was captivated by curiosity about what happened where my father worked. Somehow, I imagined great things would happen for me when I had my opportunity to join in my father's profession. Finally my father gave in to my pleading and nagging, "Please, *por favorito*, *Papacito*, take me to work with you, Daddy."

The great day began at dawn. My mother was the first one up and she made tortillas for breakfast and lunch. The sun began to show its face and I was on my way to become an orange picker. Before going to work, my older brother would get on his knees and pray. I asked my mom why he prayed and she said, "He prays to God that it rains so he won't have to go and pick oranges."

Looking back on those days, the most vivid memories I have are of the early morning rides in the back of a camper-like truck, listening to the chatter of the men who did this work day in and day out. I prayed for the orchards to be far away so that I might sleep a few more minutes.

In the winter, the trees were usually wet with the morning frost and the coldest of water would quickly seep into my gloves and shirt sleeves. Once the initial shock had been absorbed, I began picking. When I started working I was intent on picking as many boxes as I could. I was obsessed with the idea of being the fastest orange picker in my crew, particularly being faster than my father.

As noontime drew closer, the smut from the pots that burned coal to keep the fruit from freezing began to melt and cake my face black; sometimes it would find its way into my eyes. Other difficulties were cutting my finger with the clipper, stabbing my arm with a broken twig, having rotten oranges hit my face, and when climbing up the middle of a tree, broken branches scratching my face. All of this activity made the day uncomfortable and trying. It wasn't long before I too was praying for rain.

At the age of eight I began to pick regularly on weekends and during summers; this continued until I turned fifteen. I learned the art of being a coyote (that is, going ahead and scouting the trees that have the largest oranges). The larger the orange, the faster boxes were filled. The more boxes filled, the more money. There were times we picked orange groves that had trees over twenty feet tall and the oranges were as small as golf balls. I remember asking my father, "Why do we get paid such little money?" He answered, "Because we have no power, my son. Pickers have tried to organize but always the growers have broken up those efforts; perhaps someday it will come to pass, but I do not believe it will happen in my time." By the age of ten, I was consciously aware of the powerlessness orange pickers faced. There was no compensation for the disparity we faced at those groves, where the opportunity to earn a decent living was nonexistent. I did not analyze or even attempt to propose a solution to this dilemma, except to suggest walking off the job. People would then say, "And where do we go when we walk off?" I had no answer; consequently, I learned to live with hostility and helplessness. I vowed I would not pick oranges all my life. Some men would laugh and say, "You'll be picking the rest of your life, just like us." I would become very angry and repeat to myself, "I won't, I won't, I won't..."

Another facet of my childhood took place in Los Angeles, where my parents and I would go at least once a month. There we would see *variedades* and go to dinner. The entire show came from Mexico and brought great Mexican stars such as Pedro Enfante, Dolores del Rio, Pedro Vargas, Cantinflas and others. Celebrities with whom every young American identified. (I say this jokingly because most kids my age did not know who these actors were.) Romance, honor, courage and tequila became my world. Spanish was my first language and I had seen articulate and confident Mexican movie stars express their dreams, visions and beliefs. My little heart used to beat with excitement when, in battle, the *valiente* would stand up for the poor and win.

On one of these excursions, when I was about eight years old, my father said to me, "It is time you begin to learn how to find the bus station in case someday you have to get you and your mother back home." The bus was our only way to travel because my father didn't drive.

I loved being responsible for getting my mom back home and the opportunity to be in charge. Sometime after I had learned my way to the depot, we were at the show and we had seen both movies. My mother told me that my father had walked out during the last movie and he had not returned. We saw both movies one more time and when my father still did not return, my mother was very angry, "*awitada* to the max" (as we used to say in the streets). My father had told my mom that he was going out for a few moments, which turned into hours. Needless to say, the drills were over. I took a deep breath and then I took my mom by the hand and off we went. Once we began to walk I recognized the landmarks and then the depot was in sight. On the way home that evening, my mom explained to me that my father had gone out to have a beer or two and that he probably met some friends and that was the reason he had not returned. There were to be other times that my father was missing because of drinking.

I loved my father very much and I simply learned to bury my anger, rejection and disappointment when he did not show up, or when he broke his word. He was such a generous, kind, humble and wise man when he was not drinking. Early in my childhood I noticed he drank a fifth of wine or two quarts of beer every day. He called his booze "*medecina*." During the week, he never got violent; however, there were a few times he would drink on the weekends and he would try to hit my mom. She would run out to a neighbor's house and call the police. This was not a daily occurrence, but it happened enough to cause pain and hurt that I swiftly buried. At other times, my father would come home drunk from a weekend excursion and he would be disoriented, tired, smelly and injured. One time he came home beaten up; there was dried blood on his face and he smelled like vomit. It brought sickness up to my throat and then it dropped to the pit of my stomach like a rock at the bottom of the sea, never to rise again. My tears grew to great proportions, but I swallowed those tears and vowed I would never be like that.

My father had another side. He showered me with gifts and showed a genuine concern and a warmth. He taught me how to work, to respect my elders and the value of cleanliness. The paradox between the way he treated me and the way he treated himself was something that I did not understand, although I really did try. I would see him leave to get his hair cut and he looked really sharp with his polished shoes, pressed dress pants, silk shirt and a glossy, gray velour hat. When he returned, the picture was the opposite. I knew he would not allow me to be that way; for me, he always wanted the best. He once told me, "My son, if you do not ever start drinking, smoking or gambling, you will never have to worry about stopping." Advice he did not take himself.

During my early childhood, I was aware that life could be very difficult. I started school when I was five and a half; this is when I was introduced to the English language. We spoke Spanish at home so when I walked into my kindergarten class, everyone who spoke English did not make sense to me. I do not remember much about kindergarten except that if I raised my hand and pointed to the lavatory I could walk out of the classroom. On my exit, I would run away from school. It seems that my first year was spent running away from, and being returned to, school. After the initial embarrassment of flunking, the second year in kindergarten was much better, although realizing that I could not play on the playground with the first graders was painful. There were some positive aspects; I felt a sense of confidence rather than that gnawing terror I had known in the first year when I was called on to print a letter, or figure out some puzzle which I was unable to do. The second year of kindergarten was not so traumatic.

In the first grade, my teacher's name was Mrs. Finneyfrogg and she was kind and pretty. I do not remember too much about school except that all of the Mexican kids were in the lowest reading group. Before the year was over, I had been passed to the second group. Mrs. Finneyfrogg would use me as an example to the other kids in the third reading group. She would say, "Perhaps someday you too can go on the second group if you work hard." Momentarily this made me feel better than them, but then I would think, "Why can't I be in the first reading group?" At times we were given exercises in spelling or in matching various forms and figures that just frustrated me endlessly. I would envy the kids who seemed to actually enjoy those activities. I would do my best not to let anyone know how frustrated I was with my inability to perform. I really thought people were looking at me and saying how dumb I was. It seems that the harder I tried, the worse the inner pain became and the less I got done. Then, I would begin to perspire monstrous beads of sweat that soon covered my entire face and simply would not stop dripping from my nose, no matter how fast I would wipe them off. I used to think that maybe I would flunk the first grade as I had flunked kindergarten. A miracle happened; I passed the first grade and I discovered that I was speaking English. At home I spoke Spanish and with my friends I spoke a mixture of Spanish and English.

In the second grade, my friends were very important to me. My closest friends ranged in age from the fifth to the seventh grades. I hung around with a gang called "The Midnight Bandits." I never felt a real part of the gang, although I was accepted as one of the *vatos*. There was a uniform that went along with being a *vato*. It consisted of khakis, Sir Guy shirts (buttoned to the top), French toe shoes and a tattoo of a cross. I was in the third grade when I wore my first khakis and I felt like I was ten feet tall and could walk through walls. By this time I had learned to steal, lie, cheat, drink, smoke and make out with the *wisas*. The stealing was semi-organized; the *vatos* had an idea how the stores and warehouses were set up, so we could knock them off. We stole money from various sorts of vending machines, ripped off homes for appliances, and shoplifted clothing from stores.

Stealing served as a tremendous bonding force because the scheme demanded cooperation and planning for execution. I was the only third grader in the gang and the leaders were seventh graders. My duties were to be the comic and to crawl into small windows and open doors. Disneyland had opened in our hometown and we had figured out how to sneak into the park. Stealing there was easy because of the huge crowds. It was at Disneyland that I had the realization that "trouble" could come as a result of stealing. One day, someone got caught, and when the vendor called the boy out we all took off running with the Disneyland security police chasing us. I ran like I had never run in my life. I was zigzagging, knocking down trash cans and not looking back, even though I wanted to; instinct said, "Don't look back because they will see your face." Finally, I saw the fence getting closer near Fantasyland and I sprinted toward it. I hit the fence hard with my right foot, took hold of the barbed wire and swung my body over. I tore my shirt and cut my hand, but I felt I might be free. I continued to sprint to the nearby house of a friend. When I got there, Weasel and Grasshopper were already there; Duke and Bozo had gotten caught but everybody knew they would not squeal. Then my mind cried out, "Would I squeal? Could I keep my mouth shut?" My stomach had butterflies that would not quit and I prayed that no one would see how scared I was.

This scene was to replay itself many times in the next three years. Rather than recreate the scenes, I'll share the feelings that accompanied them. Although I loved being with the gang, down deep inside I suppressed a tremendous discomfort. There was a knowing and silent force which kept me aware that I did not really belong; I was different.

As the stealing increased, the arrests followed and eventually I sat in a small cell in the Anaheim town jail. There were three other guys in the cell with me and the familiar chant was being recited, "Don't squeal... don't squeal... don't squeal..." Two guys went before me and each returned with an emotionless face; they had not squealed. As I was escorted to the interrogation room, I played the part just as my *consafos* had done. My heart was beating very rapidly, but on the outside there was no expression. The questions began and so did the chant, "Don't squeal, don't squeal." I knew that I did not want to inform on anyone and that I would rather go to juvenile hall than be a "snitch", but my confidence was shaky. Those interrogations were very, very taxing because they presented the opportunity to fail as a *vato* and eventually as a man. I was ten years old and I never squealed; but, inside of me I was ashamed because of the fear I felt.

Life was to unfold in front of me as a flower does when the growing process is accelerated by trick photography. I saw my oldest brother go to San Quentin, my sister's first husband overdose on heroin, *vatos* being shot, people cutting each other and abortionists coming and going from little barrio houses. Through all of this, my mother and father begged me to change my ways. My father continued to talk, and hit me with a belt each time I was caught misbehaving. My mother cried and warned that I was going to end up in prison.

On my eleventh birthday, I ditched school and went to Santa Ana with four *vatos*. One of the guys was like my brother. In Santa Ana, we hit a few stores. I was carrying a knife and a few other gadgets I had ripped off. We began to go into cars that had open doors. Someone must have seen us and called the cops, because out of nowhere a black and white appeared. We were caught one more time. My heart began to beat as it always did and my head played that chant, "Don't squeal, don't squeal, don't squeal..." The cops took us to the Santa Ana Police Station, where we sat in a tank that was dark and covered with graffiti. In less than an hour, my *consafos* were taken away and I sat alone in that tank for over five hours. There was a small window where I could look out and see the alley. Every now and then I could see people's feet walking along the ledge. I watched the sunlight disappear into a darkness that filled my being. I began to pray and beg God to get me out of this jam. I must confess that my prayers were said in total desperation. I believed that God had given up on me a long time ago. My parents had seen to it that I continued with my catechism, but very quickly I saw inconsistencies in the Catholic religion, so I simply did not feel that God could be a friend or an ally. Yet in times of trouble, I pleaded for his helpful intervention.

13

Finally, from the dark hall a big cop came and took me by the arm, looked right through me and said, "If it was up to me, I would lock you up and throw away the key. Your sister and mother are here to pick you up." The last thing he said was, "Those punks covered for you."

On the way home I breathed a sign of relief, because once I got my spanking from my dad it would all be over. When I got home my dad said, "*Vieja*, get the boy something to eat." Then he looked at me and said, "Very early tomorrow morning I am going to tell you something." He left the room. He did not look angry or disturbed; there was no expression on his face. It was blank. Soon, beans were wrapped in my mom's homemade tortillas. That night my thoughts were on the guys that were locked up. I fell asleep thinking about prison. I had been to San Quentin twice to visit my brother and I was impressed; there was status associated with doing time. But there was no status involved in sitting in the dark, smelly tank in which I had been isolated that day.

"*Mi hijo, mi hijo, mi hijo!*" I woke to my father's voice and my heart jumped. Then I thought, "He is going to hit me now. What a burn to get a guy when he's half asleep." "*Mi hijo, no te voy a pegar.* You are a fine young man but you have learned some very bad ways. Hitting you with my belt will not help you anymore. I wish it could, but it will not. You, *mi hijo*, must decide what you want from this life. You have learned to work to care for yourself, but you persist in breaking the law. Soon you will be in prison and you must choose what you want." I felt I had broken his spirit; I felt like an arrow had been shot into my heart. It was unbelievably painful to have my father utter those words. I wanted to cry and to run to my "*papacito's*" arms but I just sat there, afraid to even hide my face. When he left the room, the tears welled in my eyes and I hated him and I hated me, but there was nowhere to go. I was determined not to end up in prison.

During this time in my life, I was consciously searching for something; I did not find what I was looking for. One day my life seemed to pass in front of me and I knew the days were numbered before I got sent away for a long time. I had seen guys jump girls and rape them; I had seen guys cut and kick each other until they were almost dead; and I had been part of a group who jumped a guy and beat him senseless. All of those times I wondered why, why did I do this? There was no answer. I never really believed I was a part of the gang. I knew even then that I was holding a part of me back and if they really knew me, they would get rid of me.

CHAPTER 3

The American Dream

There were a number of significant events that transpired after my eleventh birthday. Orange groves that once surrounded my home were disappearing; freeways had been built; and people were coming to Anaheim from all over the country. These new people were very different. They had cars, large television sets and refrigerators (full of food). I felt jealous and envious, but I accepted that there was nothing I could do about it. The *vatos* I had run with were now going to junior high, high school or doing time, so we were separated. During this year, I did not drink or blow any weed. I got into the *gabacho* (anglo) world more than I had ever done. I got more involved in sports and experienced success in all of them.

There was a great man by the name of Pinky who was the elementary schoolground coach. He radiated a very special kind of warmth that made me feel important. That year the team I was on had a great season. Pinky had bought blue and gold jerseys with our name on the backs. I think they cost a few dollars, which our parents paid. The team tied for first place. The playoff game was with St. Catherine's. They were ahead by one point with just a few seconds left. My team was a few yards away from the goal and I told Dick, our quarterback, to call an end around. I was the end and he gave me the ball. I came within a few feet of making a touchdown, but I fell short. I felt a tremendous sense of failure. I replayed that run a thousand times. One of my friends told me the guard did not pull and there was no way I could have made the touchdown without the blocking. I did not hear him. This was one more thing I could not forgive myself for.

The school district was growing and the boundaries were changed. Consequently, I went to a different junior high, which took me away from the gang. I consciously tried to stay out of reach of the police. There were times the gang came looking for me, found me, and asked me to help them with a theft or a fight. I usually was able to sidestep those requests. There was one *vato*, Ace, who was my main *consafo*. I know he kept people off my back. The guys my age wanted me to be their leader in starting a new gang. I told them, "The *movida* is over for me." About this time, Ace began to use drugs regularly. He was a bright, intelligent guy, but I knew he had made his choice. He had become a *tecato* (heroin addict).

For the next three years, I slowly learned the ways of the *gabas*. I did not know then that they were Irish, Germans, Polish, Swedes, Italians and sometimes a mixture of all these. To me, they were simply *gabas*. I concentrated my energy on sports and drama. In drama, I could become whoever I wanted to be, and sports gave me a sense of belonging. I was not fully committed and I felt my friends were. I practiced and played hard because I wanted to start, not because I loved playing. I found myself playing sports for what they could do for me socially. Nevertheless, I played well enough to be first string. I was also on the student council and received leads in the class plays. However, I always seemed to be riding an emotional roller coaster.

I did not drink any *pisto* (booze) for one year. Then in the eighth grade I found a bottle of Johnny Rebel whiskey and I got very loaded. I began to drink again, because I knew booze could "make it better".

I remember seeing the small groups of *vatos* who continued to wear their khakis and there were even some *gabas* that wore khakis. Somehow, in my mind, they were different from where I had come from. The girls I went with had never seen me when I was a *vato-loco*; they were very kind and loving to me. The girls would make sandwiches for picnics and we would "make out" all afternoon. One day on the way to meet my girlfriend, I was jumped by a group of *vatos*, who had replaced the gang I used to run with. They wanted to "rat pack" me but I told them I would take on their toughest guy. As he walked out to fight me, I ran past him. Later on that day, I saw one of the guys who jumped me and I told him to leave me alone or I would hurt him. After that day, I wasn't bothered again.

I was now in the ninth grade and that summer was to be my last year picking oranges. After graduation, I had the feeling that my girl, Patti, and I were not going to make it. Her parents had been asking her not to see me anymore because I was Mexican. Patti really felt bad about it and so did I, although this was not new to me. It had happened in the eighth grade with an Italian girl I was seeing.

Sometime that summer, I began to feel very distant from my mother and father. I was ashamed of the barrio and of the house we lived in. I could see that our house was decrepit compared to my friends' homes. When friends' parents would give me rides home, I had them drop me off in front of someone else's home in the nicer neighborhoods that were across the park from where I lived.

Reviewing my last year in junior high, I can see that it had been three years since I had been in jail. I continued, infrequently, stealing and drinking, and I experienced long periods of discomfort. This discomfort became intense when I could not see Patti anymore. I had never really experienced that kind of conscious grief. During these years, my mom had become very ill. (Come to think of it, my mom had been ill off and on most of her life; somehow, I was not affected by her illness.) When the mother of my closest friend died, his feelings about her death were mixed.

The summer was long and hot and the days were ones of isolation and despair. I found myself going to Disneyland and feeling out of place. I yearned for someone or something to fill the emptiness in my life. It was as if I were a doorway and cold wind was running through. There was no one with whom I could share these feelings. Even when I went with guys to Disneyland, I felt alone and uncomfortable. Feelings were something I did not really understand, except they could really move me way up or way down. It was like being caught in a large spider web and the more I tried to get out of the web, the worse it got. I used to think that there must be a way to not feel so bad. I couldn't stand this slow killing pain that seemed to grasp me by the throat. I determined that I was going to figure out how not to have to experience that feeling.

In the late summer, I went to a few barrio parties but I felt out of place. I was playing the part of the *vato*, but something had been lost or misplaced. The *vato loco* was inside, but I would not let him out in public. It seemed there was no place I belonged. Beer and wine began to be the answer to all the *pinche* questions I had in my head. I didn't know what was causing this discomfort, but I knew that beer and wine made it better. Summer was always more difficult than the school year; but finally school began. It was 1961 and the town had changed tremendously. There were now five high schools in Anaheim. There were freeways, defense plants, shopping malls, people and more people.

Except for three houses, the barrio I lived in was being destroyed. I could see houses being bulldozed from our kitchen window. It was just a matter of time before the iron monster would get to our home. I was indifferent to the whole mess. I had lived somewhere between the houses of three women, Mercy, Grace and Hope, and now their homes were gently evaporating into the past.

I was able to see the bulldozer leveling Mercy's house. Her home was being slowly demolished by the monstrous force called progress. Mercy was a dark lady who had seven kids. I was never really sure, but I think people said she was a Mexican Yaqui Indian from Arizona. She was a strong lady who held nothing back when she talked with men or women. Hope's house had been dusted away some time ago. All that was left was a pile of broken wood. The house on the other side of us was Grace's. This lady was a very reserved and quiet person, who had for some reason been given the honor of being called *dona*. Of the three women, Hope was the only one who spoke English and appeared to be Americanized. The barrio was disappearing fast.

Going from junior high to high school was a little scary and I thought about Patti in the early part of the year. However, when football practice started I wanted to do the best I could, so that I could be first string. I made the first defensive team and began to hang around with the guys that were a year ahead of me. It seemed that the rap focused on chicks or getting loaded when football was over.

I had a tremendous need for a girl. I always had one girl on whom I could depend. (This dependence goes back to the third grade.) I thought girls were exciting and all my girlfriends were the most beautiful creatures that God had ever created. This is how it was in my mind. I did not have a girlfriend the first three or four months of school; I was becoming desperate. I continued to take drama and I had received the Best Actor award in junior high. I came to love the feeling of receiving awards, but my joy was acting on the stage. I loved being whoever the script called for. I fell in love with my drama teacher, who was a small-boned, petite lady who had black hair, dark eyes and a way of moving that made me follow her. Nevertheless, my girl search continued as the hunt does for the hungry hawk.

Finally, she appeared, and in some ways she looked like my drama teacher, Mrs.T.; but she sure did not have Mrs.T.'s talent and spirit. What she did have was the ability to kiss and touch like no other girl I had ever known. When this girl brushed her lips over mine I felt like every nerve in my body had been electrocuted. I had had an obsession with some form of sexual experience from the time I was five or six years old, when my oldest brother asked me to sweep his kitchen. He told me he would have a reward for me when I finished sweeping. I came for my reward and he pulled down his girlfriend's blouse and there stood perfectly formed light brown breasts with dark moons and nipples at the end. My relentless and insatiable "want" for *more* began, and my relentless pursuit for "again" grew. I do not remember if I was ten or eleven, but there was a night I was with a young lady and I was rubbing against her thigh. It was flesh rubbing on flesh and it was like two lost notes finding each other in the dark mist and forming a melody that grew into a rushing and thundering rhapsody. I remember trying to hold back the final rush because I thought I was going to pee my pants; but it was impossible. I did not know I had experienced an orgasm, but I could see and feel that something had happened.

So this tenth grade girl was a goddess of lovemaking, but she did not really care for me. She seemed to be interested in older guys. Her parents were from the South and they had great misgivings about my last name and the color of my skin. We had a date one night, but she had to break it, so she had a friend of hers go in her place. Her friend, Carol, and I had been buddies, so it worked out well. We went to see *West Side Story*. The movie was spectacular and served as a perfect lubricant for falling in love. Carol and I began a relationship that went on for two years. I was not an experienced lover. I just was persistent in trying to re-experience that excitement I had felt when I was eleven. Once I had secured a relationship, I was able to look toward the future. Before the tenth grade ended, I had made up my mind that I was going to be the first Mexican student body president of my school.

It was a successful yet painful year. I played first string football on the B championship team; I had supporting roles for all the school's plays and received "Best Supporting Actor" (in Orange County). I was in all the assemblies and Spring Flings. I was very fortunate to participate in activities that made my face and name popular. I had become very visible and I knew that was going to help when I ran for student body president. Most of my acquaintances were juniors or seniors, though I did have a few close friends in my own class. I met a friend, John, who liberated me from the orange groves and introduced me to the dry cleaning business. My pal John had run for student body president and lost. John was the poorest *gabacho* I had ever known and he reminded me of a *vato* more than anyone I had met in a long time.

The pain came when Carol's parents refused to let her date me anymore. They too, were threatened by my ethnic background. I had learned to rationalize rejection many years ago but the knot in my stomach got larger and a little tighter. The summer came and I worked in the cleaners and learned to clean clothes and do a little pressing. I saw my girl when she was able to sneak out with girlfriends or one of my friends would take her out and bring her to me.

The summer went by in a flash. The junior year began and I continued to play football and run track, and I was very active in drama. I worked on weekends and opened the cleaners at 7:00 each morning. I swept down the sidewalk each morning and watched the kids drive their cars to school. I had bought a cherry maroon '37 Dodge for 200 dollars. It made me angry that I had to work, but I knew that working was part of my life. It paid for the food, the clothes and the booze.

That year, a guy who worked in the cleaners with me strangled his girlfriend and then killed himself. They left a note asking to be buried side by side. This guy's dad was a cop and they were afraid to tell their parents that she was pregnant. I was stunned that this had happened but I avoided giving the matter much thought. I had noticed that a lot of crazy things happened and no one seemed able to stop them.

That year the bulldozer was flirting with our home and my parents had been given a warning that they had to move. They chose to move to Los Angeles, but there was no way I was going to leave Anaheim. Before the year was over, I moved out. My mother sobbed and begged me not to leave. My father said, "It's time for him, Lupe. He is a man and it is his turn to meet life." This man astounded me at times. I made my break and went out to meet life, and she was waiting for me. I saw life as a "she" because I saw beauty as feminine and life at her best was beautiful.

Once I left home, I did not visit much. I had to prove to myself that I did not have to ask for help. The junior year was coming to an end and I received more awards in drama, football, etc., and the election for student body president was before me. My main competitor had been the sophomore and junior class president and his dad had a reputable position in the school district. I had a couple of guys, Richard and Paul, who helped me make posters. They knew that I had planned on this for a long time. These two guys had been by me most of my life and they had grown up in "el otro barrio", the other village, which was called "La Fabrica". We walked and rode to school and parties together and each of us had developed a group we hung with at school. But we seemed to end up together when we really needed each other.

The elections were just a few days away and my opponent had many more and much larger posters than I did, so Richard and Paul decided to rip off some long poles from a restaurant to make a large poster. They were busted and their parents had to pick them up at the police station. Richard called me that evening to let me know what had happened. We ended up laughing because I could have been with them. The future student body president could have ended up in jail before he ever got elected.

The assembly prior to election took place and the mother of my opponent introduced him. Then my turn came and Richard introduced me. This introduction was a real sacrifice that my friend made for me because, although he was an all-league football player and he was extremely well known, he did *not* like to speak to large crowds. But he did it for me. Election day had come to an end and the results were not in. I was not sure if I was going to win, but I was sure that I wanted to. I think I even whispered a short prayer. The former student body president came out and announced that I had won. I felt a tremendous rush. Someone whispered that I had received over 70 percent of the votes. It was an exciting rush that lasted a few seconds. Then Mr. B., the student government adviser, came over and congratulated me and then said, "Student body president is a very demanding position and I hope you live up to it. I really believe Joe was more qualified." Once the rush was over, I ran to the cleaners and told Jess, who was like my mentor. By the time I got to my pad, the rush was over. The next few days there were many people congratulating me, yet I could not accept their good wishes because I felt unworthy. I felt depressed and I didn't know why, except that somehow, I believed these people really would not like me if they really knew me. I felt very alone and empty.

Stability was missing from my life. I had lived with an eighty-two year old lady for three or four months, then with John's family. His mom was a very kind and accepting person. Then I had moved to a place that belonged to one of the orange grower's sons, Pete. Pete became a somewhat close friend. He, like John, had something that drew us together. Even though Pete's parents were rich, he was hurting and I knew it. I lived there for six or eight months and then his dad made everyone move out.

I looked forward to the weekends because I knew I could get so loaded that I could see triple. There were many times before I took my first drink that I could consciously dream of drinking as much as I could so I could get drunk as possible without passing out, and it was then that I could see triple. At the time, I found it enjoyable. I loved getting totally wasted. I felt like I was walking on the edge of life and I would never fall off.

Carol and I were fighting more than ever now. We cared for each other, but it was trouble looking for a place to happen. It had been over a year that we had been sneaking out. Our relationship had become a series of breakups and then going back together. It was almost as if we were addicted to each other, because our times together had become painful and sad, but we simply could not let go. That next summer I did not see her. I moved into an apartment with Jess and Paul, John's older brother. Paul was not anything like John, but he was a very good example for me because he was going to college. Jess was about fifteen years older than me and he was a Mexican. He had grown up with *gabas*, or at least he did not have the quality that I had decided made somebody real *raza* or part of the mythical *vida loca*.

I was able to live that summer in a semblance of comfort because booze - V.O., Tanqueray, Calvert and good old wine - had become my love. A substitute for the dependence I had on girls and the insatiable obsession to achieve, to succeed, to attempt to fill up this empty feeling of worthlessness that seemed to continuously emerge.

As senior year began, I played student body president as I had played the ragpicker in *Madwoman of Chaillot* or Tajamura, the Japanese bandit in *Gates of Rashomon*. It was a role. But I must say, I wanted to play it better than anyone ever had.

Sports became a total disaster. They had become a burden to me because they got in the way of my drinking; so I rationalized them away. I dropped out of football a week or two before the season ended and I did the same with track.

I did very well in drama that year and I received Best Actor in an Orange County drama tournament, but something was beginning to slip away. Mrs. T. became very angry with me one day and told me, "Why can't you be more responsible? Don't you know I have picked these plays centered around your strengths, and then you don't show up when you're needed?"

In addition, Carol and I were fighting more than ever. I got very angry one night and slammed my fist through my windshield. I was beginning to get intense attacks of "uneasiness" and I had no idea what was happening.

That year, President Kennedy had been shot and while at school the word came that he had died. Our play was delayed so that we could mourn. I remember Michelle, one of my friends, coming into the student cabinet room and announcing that President Kennedy had been shot. She began to cry. I thought of my mother and how she had said that Kennedy was for the Mexican people. I was stunned, and once again I sidestepped the feelings.

The year moved on like a leaf floating down the river and soon graduation was before me. I worked on my graduation speech enthusiastically, feeling as if I were riding the crest of divine inspiration. I hungered to achieve something in that speech; I did not know exactly what. My mother, father, and brother Victor, I knew, were coming to the graduation ceremonies. When the speech was written, I practiced until I had it memorized. I remember the annuals had come out and my picture was plastered full length on one of the front pages. I knew then that this exposure was what I sought; but again I did not know why.

On graduation day, I had become somewhat still inside. When the ceremony started I became calm and knew I was ready to give my final high school performance. Then someone announced my name and as I walked up to the podium I saw my family; my mother, father, brother, sister and her husband, my aunt and my two cousins. I reached the podium and I waited a few seconds as I looked over the audience before I began. Instinct told me this is how you set the stage and set the mood. I felt like I had the morning my father had refused to spank me. I'm not sure if these were my words, but this is the message I believe I delivered. "America is a country of communities made up of families just like us. We, the Class of '64, go on to a life that waits for us with open arms. You, our parents, have set a stage for us and now we must walk on it. I beseech you and my classmates to remember that America must include all communities that make her up; the poor, the rich, the black, the brown, the yellow and the red. It is time for this to happen. I commit that this class will make this a reality." I returned to my seat. There were a thousand tears stirring in my soul and I refused to allow one to escape. Someone whispered, "That was great." I looked up and saw my *jefito* (pop). He was wearing gray slacks, shirt and hat. He also wore dark glasses. This was my first activity he had ever come to. I swallowed the tears, the joy, the ecstasy, and allowed alienation to surface and dominate my being. After the ceremony, I went up to my family. They were all very proud. Victor, my brother, had often brought my mom to see me perform on stage and he had gone to all of my performances. I was not aware then of how much that meant to me. I went behind the bleachers to hug my parents. That night I did not drink. I felt empty.

The summer of '64 began with a crisis. I found out Carol had been making out with the friend who picked her up for me. I was hurt, but I knew that no matter what happened, the "juice" would get me by.

That summer was a blur. I do not know when the hangovers began, but by this time they were horrible. It seems I always woke up deathly ill with my mouth walled with dry vomit, cuts and scratches all over my body, shakiness and an unbearable nausea that caused my insides to scream in discomfort. I would just hold on and pray for it to pass. It usually took most of the day. I remember a few times staying up all night, spending most of the time throwing up. I would go to work sick. Then Jess would say, "Why don't you take a nap, kid?" I would lie down and the whole room swam around. I was uncomfortable lying down or standing up. It was just hell. Eventually I would fall asleep.

I began summer school at a junior college since I had decided to go on with my education. I took an American history course and got a B grade in it. I desperately wanted to pass, for the obsession to achieve was still alive. I wanted to prove something to "them".

I had arranged to work thirty hours a week and take three courses a year at a community college. I ran for Commissioner at Large, because I had learned that these positions provided "special privileges" and a way into the System. I won the election and became Commissioner at Large. Because my parents lived in Los Angeles, I lied about my residency in order to attend a local junior college. Then I began to look for a girl that would accompany my "juice" and my great escape. It seemed like every girl I asked out rejected me. They just did not want to get involved with me. I was lonely and I felt ugly. I began to talk to this girl in psych class, who was out of the student government and social group with whom I spent my time. I schemed, lied, turned on the charm and did everything to gain this girl's trust. Finally, she fell. I knew that she was just temporary, until I found "Susie Creamcheese." This lady, Marsha, was kind, generous, and very giving. She came from a town called Beaver Falls, and she said she knew Joe Namath. She was a studious person and wanted to become a registered nurse. One night I was at her pad and a drunk totaled my car while it was parked out front. I began to borrow her car to take out other girls. When the academic year came to an end, I was on academic probation. That summer of '65 was to hold some surprises for me.

CHAPTER 4

Disparity and Marriage

I had concluded a full year of college and was off academic probation. I was able to raise my grade point average to exactly a 2.0 by cramming for finals. That spring semester, I slipped into an English course by mistake and I was attracted by the exuberance and dedication that the instructor had in teaching writing and literature. I didn't understand all that he was saying, but I felt inspired by his enthusiasm. At the third session of class, he told me he appreciated the comments I had made, but I had to successfully pass English 60 (Dumbbell English) before I could enroll in his course. He said, "I sure would like to have you in my class next semester; you're a fine student." From that moment on, I knew I would be in his course the next fall.

I didn't pass English 60 during the spring term because I didn't do the work. I detested grammar and it seems I got drunk on the eve of quizzes and exams. Finally, during summer school, I managed to stay sober long enough to pass. I decided before summer school started to try out for yell leader. Seven guys were selected. I had tremendous desire to belong and to be active. Also, I loved excitement and attention, and yelling seemed like it would be a blast! There was another guy on the squad who liked to drink the way I did. The next year was set if I could keep my grade level at 2.0. I went to summer school to insure the latter.

At summer school, I met a guy who had fought some of the guys I grew up with. He had been a *vato* and we had a lot to share. He wanted to become a policeman and I was thinking about being a probation officer. We spent the evenings after class drinking in bars. He was three or four years older; I was twenty years old at the time. For a few months, we rapped about the past and what we were going to do in the future. We both wanted to add something positive to our communities. We decided all we could do was try.

Then the world caved in on me and I felt like every bone in my body had been crushed. I received a call from the Los Angeles County Hospital.

My father was there and he had been badly hurt. Walking through the gigantic building, passing rooms that cried out with pain from the patients that lay in them, my brother Vic and I located my dad. He was swollen all over and he could not speak clearly; his words were slurred and mumbled. He looked like someone had beaten him with a baseball bat. We were told to return in two weeks, when a hearing would be held to determine his mental status.

Two weeks later, my brother and I were listening to a court-appointed psychiatrist reporting my father was suffering from chronic syphilitis. The blow of that word "syphilis" left me breathless and as my breathing returned I screamed inwardly, NO, NO, NO! My father, my pop, was committed to Metropolitan State Mental Hospital for the remainder of his life. I wanted to kill, but there was no one to attack. I just swallowed hard. I was very confused about my feelings and I didn't know who to talk to. At the same time, I was afraid and ashamed to talk to anyone about my feelings. I do remember Jess, my roommate, telling me about his dad and his family. Jess always seemed like he was so well put together. Invincible. In fact, most people I knew appeared very strong and stable compared to how I felt and thought of myself. Alcohol deadened the pain and allowed me to cry for myself and for my dad. I felt we both had failed.

Vic and I went to visit my dad and he was slowly beginning to wither away. His speech was totally incoherent and eventually he would just sit there and stare out into space. God, I loved him so much and yet there was another feeling at the bottom of my gut that produced hate for my poor old dad. The feeling was very confusing and it felt like I was being strangled with rage and sorrow at the same time. I was hurt and frightened, so I simply withdrew into my medicine, alcohol, the sleeper. Something had happened to my insides and I didn't know exactly what it was except that I was drinking to forget and to bury what was inside of me. I didn't talk about what I was feeling because I wasn't really aware.

As the school year began, I trained with the yell squad and my friend from yesterday went on his way. I was not involving Marsha in my social life because I was ashamed of being seen in public with a girl that did not look like a fox. I was very mixed up about these feelings of social insecurity. What would people say about her being a little heavy? I knew my brother Vic, Jess, and other friends liked her, but I was ashamed. However, I led her on because I wanted her company and affection and I was afraid to be alone. I would talk to Marsha for hours and tell her about the past and about all the dreams I had and the dreams the booze would make up as I went along. I felt like I loved her when I was loaded and flying high. She seemed to feel that way about me all the time. When school started in the fall, I didn't see Marsha during the week.

There was a dance coming up after the first week of school. I knew the song leaders would be there and I hoped I was going to end up with one of them. I thought I would find "Suzie Creamcheese" and everything would be okay.

I drank two or three quarts of beer before the dance, with a few hits of hard booze, and jumped into the '58 Studebaker Lark. When I got to the dance, I was buzzing. I saw this small framed girl standing next to one of the song leaders and I asked her to dance. We danced four or five dances. She was a fabulous dancer. I took her outside for a walk. I was soaking wet from perspiration. We talked endlessly and in the course of this euphoric exchange, I discovered she was Mexican American, although I believe she accentuated her Spanish heritage. She was in the process of ending her high school romance and I had a feeling I was going to marry this mighty little lady who spoke with determination.

I memorized her phone number. I called her every day and eventually I told Marsha I didn't want to see her anymore. Marsha had gone on a diet to please me and she was angry when I gave her the news. She threw things at me and called me a liar and a lowdown creep. She would come to my apartment and scream at me. Finally, Marsha gave up and disappeared from my life.

By this time, I had buried my dad's situation and I was absolutely in love with this little Mexican American girl who I called Sibbers. She had been a cheerleader for three years at her high school. I took her everywhere with me and everywhere we went I drank alcohol. She found this peculiar, but she soon came to accept it.

During the fall of 1965, the armed service deferments were being dropped so I decided to join the Naval Reserves. I remember driving to Los Alamitos to be sworn in. A guy in one of my drama classes had clued me in to the opportunity. I took the oath and returned home that evening wondering what I had done and wondering if Sibbers would wait for me. I talked to her that night and she didn't seem to feel as strongly about me as I did about her. After talking to her, I drank and began to think about my dad and mom.

I had not talked to my mom for some time because I blamed her for my dad's condition. One night, I went to her house in Los Angeles after I had drunk all night and had taken some speed. I was speeding on the freeway and my vision was very blurry. I got to her house and no one was there, so I broke a window to get in. I turned on a light and became sober for a moment. I knew where I was and it terrified me to feel that insensible emptiness. In a rage I shattered my graduation picture she had next to her bed. I hated and blamed her because she was having an affair while my dad was going crazy. I left her house in a state of insanity that night, and my sobbing made it almost impossible for me to breathe. I was able to get my car started and my body was shaking uncontrollably as I drove onto the freeway.

The police stopped me somewhere on the Santa Ana Freeway. The cops were just asking me to get out of the car when they got a call on their radio. They told me to pull off the freeway and sleep it off. I stayed in my car until the cops left, then I went to a bar where there were dancing go-go girls. I felt very lonely and I wanted to be with one of those girls. I guzzled the beer down, but somehow it wasn't enough. The pain continued and the uneasiness increased. After the bar closed, I drove to Crescent Bay in Laguna Beach.

I spent the night there writing poems on the sand. My tears flowed in peace and finally a sense of calm entered my world for a few moments. When dawn arrived, my body began to tremble, and I felt a sickness I had never known. I started to drive home but I felt lost. All I remember is driving into a large wooden roadblock, which was set up to prevent cars from driving onto an unfinished freeway overpass. I was shocked as I slammed into the roadblock and I automatically put the car in reverse and raced away from the scene. Somehow I got home, but I couldn't stop throwing up. There was blood in the vomit and I was on my knees looking at the blood as I embraced the toilet. Sibbers came over that day and made soup for me.

There had been numerous nights when I became blindly intoxicated but I concealed this from Sibbers as much as possible. Her family was large, Catholic, and from a type of Mexican culture that I had never known. The family was very close and affectionate. Her dad loved to drink, tell war stories, and be surrounded by his three daughters. I became a frequent visitor of the household and I felt as accepted as someone like me could. I compared the house, the furniture and all of the material things this family had and concluded that they were much superior to my family. I wanted what they had, yet I put them down because I believed I could never have it. At that time Vic seemed to be the only family I had.

Vic had a small gathering and my mom was there. When I walked in she came running to embrace me. She was very happy to see me. I loved her and had come to the realization that she had the right to her life. I had not talked to my mom for almost a year. I believed that she was responsible for the misery in my life. I felt immense anger and disgust because she had abandoned my father. One night in a drunken stupor I was putting her down when a friend of mine said, "When was the last time you saw your dad?" Suddenly I realized that I was rejecting my mother for not seeing my dad, when I was doing the same thing. I had not seen my dad for over a year and I remember wanting to have more of my brother Victor's attention. I was confused about my feelings and expectations regarding my brother. Sometimes I cried because I felt so much for him and at other times I hated him because he could not give me more. I spent more time with my brother than I ever had and he made it clear that he was there for me; all I had to do was ask. I was just too proud to ask. I was trying to make it on my own, so I would withdraw and try to refocus my goals. I wanted to graduate from college and my grades were low. Somehow, I was able to stop drinking long enough to pass some very important courses. I had decided against drama as a major, because I could not handle the rejection of my 'new' drama teacher and I saw no chance of success. I had chosen to major in sociology and be a probation officer. There were still some very tough courses to pass, such as geology, biology and economics. These courses had to be passed in order for me to be able to go on to a state college.

I had learned to appreciate philosophy from my friend Mr. Henderson, an English professor. I read and reread Sartre and Camus, always leaving those writings with a determination to go on living no matter what, and to somehow pass those required courses. When finals came for biology and economics, I literally locked myself in my apartment for two days and studied day and night. I felt drained and futile inside. I thought perhaps there was no reason or purpose to this bloody life, but then I would look forward to the next weekend with Sib, and my booze. Before the year ended, Sib tried out for cheerleader and made it. I experienced a tremendous jealousy because I thought I might lose her.

I had experienced this fear of losing her once before when she ran for campus queen, but the intensity had never been so great. I was never really sure if I was good enough for her. I remember one night we were going to see Ray Charles at the Forum and I forgot about the concert. I got home an hour before I was supposed to pick her up. She called me and almost died because I was drunk. We went to see Ray anyway, and that night I told her she had no idea what it was like to be poor. I told her she was an upper class Mexican and she really didn't care for me. She said I was wrong and I wanted to believe her, but somehow I just couldn't.

The school year came to an end. I had worked hard and concentrated on my studies for the realization of my dream, which was to someday graduate from a state college and be able to help the delinquents of our society. Somehow I was able to pass the difficult solid courses and was accepted at the state college. I went to boot camp, for the Naval Reserves, that summer and I couldn't drink or see Sib for two weeks. Somehow I managed to get by for those fourteen days. They cut all my hair off. I remember one guy got caught with a cigarette in his pocket and they made him eat it. There were a few guys who didn't make it. I made a few buddies during that two weeks. These were guys I had known during the Naval Reserve weekends.

When I got back home, I asked Sib to marry me and she said she wasn't ready. I felt absolutely lost with her reply, but I just stood my ground and told her she was my life. Around this time, her parents moved to a house in Orange that had a pool in the backyard. I felt more inferior after this happened; Sib stayed by my side. I was enchanted as could be.

During the past year, I had become friends with a Polish guy who was as intense about life as I was. His name was Roy and he was a very dependable friend. Roy made up his mind he wasn't going to Vietnam even if it meant leaving the country. We spent a lot of time talking about the injustices of the world. We decided somehow we would help to make it better.

I was working in Santa Ana at a cleaners because when I returned from boot camp, my boss of six years had given my job to someone else. I went mad the morning I came back to work and found someone else at my work space. I stood motionless for what seemed like an eternity. I felt like someone had hit me on the forehead with a baseball bat. I could not breathe but finally I caught my breath, ran to my car and raced to my boss's house. When he came to the door I screamed, "Why, Joe? Why did you take my job away?" He told me that he didn't think I was coming back from boot camp. I swore I would dance on his grave. I was filled with disgust and unadulterated hate for this man. I was terrified since I had never been out of a job and I wasn't sure anyone would hire me. I found a job in a few days.

That fall semester went by very rapidly. State college was challenging, but I was burnt out and seemed to be in a gray lull. I continued to drink and stay up late. People were going off to Vietnam and I knew I was going soon.

I spent that Christmas Eve with Sib and her family. They had accepted me, or at least it appeared that way. A month later Sib told me that she thought she was pregnant. She was scared and so was I. A few more days went by and she called me and told me everything was okay. I told her it would be a good idea if she went to the doctor. She went and the verdict was yes; she was pregnant. I was scared, and at the same time grateful. She talked of going to South Dakota and having the baby and giving it up for adoption. We had driven up high on a knoll and we could see north Orange below us. I listened to her and then I said, "Let's get married, Sib." She agreed. She was eighteen years old.

We talked to her mom who cried and murmured some words like, "We know you are a nice boy and you will take care of..." She suggested we not tell her dad the truth. That night, I went to ask permission from Sib's dad to marry his daughter. I told him I loved his daughter very much and that I was going overseas in a few months and I wanted Sib to have my name.

He said, "Why don't you wait until you come back?" I said, "If I die, I want to die married to her." I believed those words as I said them. He gave me his permission.

We had a lovely wedding. Sib looked as lovely as a rose in full bloom. All of our friends were there. Victor was my best man and Roy was an usher. Earlier that year, we had gone to a girl's reception who was heiress to millions of dollars, but we thought our reception was just as grand. My family was there, or at least part of it was: my Aunt Lucy, my sister Vera and her husband, Tony, and my mom. My mom was sad. She looked so lonely that day and she sat with tears trickling down her face. She was such a little lady, yet she always seemed like such a giant to me. I watched her for a moment and I wanted to run to her and put my head on her lap like I did when I was a little boy.

Sib and I left the reception early and returned to the apartment where Jess and I had lived. Sib and I were going to live there for a few months before I got my Navy orders. The next morning Sib got very sick at Mass, because of the baby, and she passed out. She looked so delicate and so innocent as I picked up her limp body. She came to and we went home. I went to work the next day and when I came home I asked Sib, "What am I supposed to do?" She said, "Sit down until dinner is ready and have a beer, that's what my dad does". At the end of the month, I received my orders to report to Long Beach Naval Base.

CHAPTER 5

Vietnam

This was a time when the notion of God was being questioned. There seemed to be much questioning about the direction that life was taking in our country. When I entered the Navy, these questions were left on campuses and lonely Southern California beaches. A number of my friends had been to Vietnam and on their return the word was "shit", there was nothing like it in the world and I was lucky to be in the Navy and not a combat soldier. I was grateful for this somewhat questionable good fortune.

I was now at Long Beach naval port waiting for orders. The word was out that River Patrol Boats, RPBs, were bad news. No one knew where they were going and there was an unsettling feeling running through my friends and myself. It seemed to me we realized that death was before us and yet we had to try to have the ability to laugh at the circumstances, and to be daring while we waited for our destiny to unfold.

Every morning we had to muster (that's the time when attendance is taken), and then we were assigned work details. One of my buddies thought of the idea that we develop our own work detail, the "Dog Tag Detail." Every morning for three weeks, we marched off to where dog tags were made. However, we never stopped at the dog tag office. Instead, we would march to the gym to play tennis, basketball, drink beer, shoot pool, or whatever else met our "wants." Our scam was discovered a week before we received our orders and we cleaned out heads for the last five days of temporary active duty.

We all had heard that River Patrol Boat was the most dangerous duty a sailor could get, next to being a corpsman with the Marines. Most of us were aware of this, because we had chosen the Navy to stay out of combat. The word was, guys I knew were being sent to destroyers (tin cans), guided missile destroyers - and two of the guys I ran with got River Patrol Boat duty. My orders were for the deck force of the U.S.S. *Higbee* (DD806), a ship that had been commissioned four months before I was born, January 27, 1945. The *Higbee* was the first, and only, American warship to be named in honor of a woman, Lenah S. Higbee, who was superintendent of the Navy nurse corps during World War I.

When I received my orders, I drank most of the day. I was able to go through the night at home in neutral, or at least I felt that way. The emotions had been smothered one more time. Saying farewell to my wife seemed less intense than I had expected. I guess it was like a dream because a part of me didn't believe, or accept, that soon I would be gone. I lived for the moment and nothing more, and soon it was time to leave for Vallejo, California where I was to board my ship.

When I landed in San Francisco, the experience was earthshaking, because for the first time it hit me that I was going someplace where I had never been. I could hear the music and the words of the song, "When you go to San Francisco, be sure to wear a flower in your hair." I was wearing a "Dixie cup" (a sailor's hat) on my hair and flowers were nowhere to be found.

I finally got to my ship; it was in drydock being repaired. We were to be in Vallejo for a month or so and then we were off to Long Beach. I flew home once from Vallejo and I almost missed that one because I missed a pay call. A few of the guys heard about my bad luck and they got together and loaned me the money for airfare. I had become depressed on payday as I was chipping paint and being bossed around by people who appeared to be so ignorant. Yet these people controlled my life. I had come to believe the statement, "Your soul belongs to Jesus, but your ass belongs to the U.S. Navy." My ass belonged to a first class boatswain's mate by the name of Mellis, who behaved like he had eternal hemorrhoids and constipation. He was an old salt who had been in the Navy all of his life. He used to say, "I was in the real Navy, when ships were made of wood and the men were made of steel." I felt like I was going to be with this old man the rest of my life.

On the night before the ship left for Long Beach, I drank into the early morning hours. I went to my rack and before long I was being yelled at to hurry up and report to the fantail; the ship was under way. I was paralyzed for a moment, as thought struck me, that I had never been on a ship at sea and I had the second watch! My stomach was experiencing a new terror - a hangover and seasickness at the same time. It was all I could do not to throw up. Finally, my watch came up and I was at lookout on the bridge on the port side. I wanted to die. Instead of dying, I just faked passing out and I was sent to my rack for the rest of the day.

For the next three months, the crew trained off San Diego for the mission off the coast of Vietnam. Most of the guys on the deck force were eighteen to twenty years old. There was a large number of guys from New England. They were really proud of being from that area. An *"esprit de corps"* was developing among us; yet I felt I was on the fringe of that experience.

A month before the ship set out for Vietnam, we returned from San Diego to our home port, Long Beach. On that day, I hitchhiked back home and got a ride from a guy who had a fifth of tequila, which we polished off by the time I got home. I was delighted to see my wife. I really wanted to be home when the baby was born. The next morning, Sib told me the baby began to kick and move in the early hours. It took a bit of time for Sib to wake me up; but finally I came to and took her to the hospital. Sib was in labor for some hours and I was fighting a very bad hangover. I was a little shaky but I knew it would pass, as it had hundreds of times before. I just wanted the baby and Sib to be okay. The lovely miracle was born and we named her Michelle Beth. Right after Michelle was born, the nurse showed her to me and I looked at this little infant. For a brief moment, I saw and felt my life in this little miracle. I then went to see Sib, who was sleeping. She had a warm smile on her face and she appeared peaceful. I wanted to jump up and down, but instead I called Sib's mother and told her the good news. In a day or two the baby and Sib were home at her mother's, safe and sound. I felt a deep sense of gratitude.

A month later, it was time to head for the coast off Vietnam. On that day, I had Sib drive me to the front gate of the Long Beach Naval Port. I didn't want her to see my ship leave. I remember kissing her goodbye and then walking off. I wanted to cry, but I stuffed the feelings. I loved her and the baby so much, but I had to hold on and not break down.

On November 3, 1967, the *Higbee* left for her tour of "search and rescue" stations off North Vietnam. As the ship pulled away, I sat on the fantail watching the buildings get smaller in the City of Long Beach. Finally, the buildings were gone and I wondered for a moment would I return. Quickly I forgot that thought and returned to my compartment.

We were under way and I was lying on my rack, when a lady ran by. I thought "What the hell is going on here?" A few minutes later, the word was out: a lady stowaway had been discovered. There were many stories of what she was going to do for her free passage to Hawaii. This was an omen of what was to follow the next six months. For example: we were almost bombed by our own airplanes; we collided with one of our refueling ships; and we sank a helicopter type instrument called "dash." The following lyrics from the "Ode to the *Higbee*", written by Willie D. Rogers and Terry E. Sloat, aptly describe the experiences we had.

(Sung to the tune of "Ode to Billy Joe")

It was the third of November on another breezy Long Beach day,
I was out holding sweepers before the ship was to get under way,
And at breakfast time, we started back to the ship for a bite to eat,
And Mellis hollered off the fantail, "Y'all remember to wipe your

feet."

He said, "We just got the news this morning from Comderson 3,
And it seems that West Pacific is the destination of the Hig-Bee."
Now Moser said to Allen as he passed around the wardroom peas,
"Kenny Groth never had a lick of sense, pass the biscuits please,"
It seems like Josephine, the stowaway, is all they ever talk about
now,
And Allen said it was a shame it had to happen anyhow,
Because lately "R" division seems to be just a little on edge,
And they tell me Kenny Groth is going to jump off the Higbee bridge.
Now Benny Boats said he recollected when he and Allen and Lanny Jo,
Were on the bridge standing watch when they heard a big bomb explode,
And wasn't I in my rack when I heard the awful noise that night,
And then I heard all three alarms go off, you know, somehow,
it doesn't seem right,
And as I saw the chunks of shrapnel that had landed on the starboard
ledge,
I saw the panic-stricken faces of the people on the Higbee bridge.
Now Billy Graves said to Powell, "Child, what's happened to your
appetite?"
They been cooking all day and you haven't touched a single bite,
That nice young corpsman, Doc Duplantis, dropped by today,
and he left you some Dramamine to take - oh, by the way,
He said he saw someone that looked a lot like you on the starboard
edge.
And it looked like you were throwing something lumpy off the Higbee
bridge.
Now a year has come and gone since we left the yards in old Frisco,
But since our run-in with the Bellatrix, it looks like we never did go.
A boatswain name of Twiggy said he saw the sparks that flew that
night,
And the Captain said he saw the port anchor as it dropped out of
sight,
And now there's no time for picking flowers up on Choctaw Ridge,
Cause now I'm busy standing port and starboard watches on the Higbee
bridge.
And I recall the Sunday Terry Kimsey took the Dash out to play,
We were steamin' up by Wanson on another cold Korean day,
The bird, it took a dive, hit the water, it'll sink I fear,
But Puckett said, "Don't sweat it child, it's got a special floatation
gear",
The old Lena swung around, they said a whaleboat recovery,

35

But now our flotation gear is floating down at the bottom of the sea,
And now there's lots more time for PMS up on the hanger scene,
Y'know, it serves 'em right for flyin' during Holiday Routine.

During this time, I saw a shipmate busted for having booze hidden in his locker. As they were taking his bottles out and breaking them in a large trash can, tears began to flow from his eyes. Someone said this guy was an alcoholic. There was another guy who drank a lot. This man had been in the "real war" (World War II). He had been a chief and now he was demoted to a third class petty officer. I drank with him and enjoyed listening to his stories of yesterday. I thought to myself, "He's no alcoholic. If he's one then I'm one and I know I'm not one." It seems like we would just get into a port and then it was time to go back to sea.

There were days out at sea when life became easy and peaceful. On those days, the realization that my life was at the government's discretion added to the absurdity of the deaths that permeated the air. I could see the helicopters flying over the hospital ships off the coast of Da Nang and I saw the marines who had lost arms and legs, and whose spirits had been broken. Paradoxically, there were days at sea of tranquility. During that time I developed a few close friendships, but somehow they didn't seem to last. David M. was the only other Chicano on the ship. He had been in the Navy four years. His reenlistment came as a result of failure to find work outside of the service. There were times when we were out at sea that we would spend day after day bombarding and I learned to fall asleep as the thunder of the explosions sang, one after another. One such day, I woke up because I thought I was dreaming that we were shooting. It was reality, not a dream. I was on this ship and I was responsible for handling ammunition that was used for bombardment. I was paralyzed with the thought of the absurdity of war, but this thought passed and I just did my time.

Once we had been out at sea for some forty days and we came into Sasebo, Japan. It was late at night and all of us in my group were drunk. Suddenly, we were all being escorted back to the ship. In the morning when I came to, the word was out that the Koreans had stolen a U.S. intelligence ship, the U.S.S. *Pueblo*. It was a very unsettling time because the word was our ship was supposed to go in after the *Pueblo*. There was a call for volunteers and no one was volunteering. There were lots of other ships in the area, including Russian ships, and we could all see each other. No mail was coming in and no mail was going out. We were just waiting for orders. The story was that the *Enterprise* would provide air support as we towed the *Pueblo* out. Of course this never happened, but the mood and those hours waiting to see what was going to happen were gray.

My job was to run the ship's store and so I spent a lot of time listening to guys tell me about their hometown or concerns they had about their future. I also was Master of Ceremonies for the ship's smoker, which was like a talent show. I was very visible on the ship as I had been at high school. I had been somewhat close, yet there was a shell that protected me from others. Most of the crew were reserves and had no investment in the Navy except to do the time and get the hell out. As we were returning to the States, Dave M. and I sat drinking three nights in a row. I had the keys to the locker where the booze was stored, and the keys to the Coke machine. It became one big party. The hangovers that followed were horrendous. The eve of the ship's arrival home, there was one last party. The next morning Dave and another sailor were shaking me, trying to bring me to. Finally, I got up and with their help I got my clothes on and went upstairs to open the ship's store. There was a line a mile long of sailors waiting to buy their wives and loved ones presents that had been forgotten while on the cruise.

I had talked to my wife once while I was in Japan and I had felt strange. I had run out of words to share and the distance I felt while talking to her was startling. Yet I wanted to be with her. She wrote me regularly and sent me pictures of her and the baby. I fantasized being with her and the fantasy was very gratifying. Now I was only a few miles away from Long Beach and I was returning home. Long Beach was in sight and for a moment, my mind was in a state of reflection. I guess, in a very silent way, I had accepted the possibility of never coming back home. Those were very crazy days when we heard the Vietcong had come into Saigon and that there was no telling if we would ever go home. All of a sudden it hit me, "Where was everybody?" It was like the whole experience had never happened. The marines and sailors who had been wounded and the ones who were walking around in shock, all appeared in front of my eyes, and then I just swallowed and swore to forget.

The ship moved into Long Beach Harbor and the families began to board as soon as the ship moored. I searched for my wife and the minutes seemed like hours as my quest found no one. I marched to my rack hopelessly, then a guy came running up to me and said, "Your wife and kid are on the fantail waiting for you." I sprinted up a ladder and ran toward the fantail. I saw her, the baby and my sister-in-law; my mother-in-law embraced me. I kissed my wife and the encounter was awkward. I felt strange and uncomfortable for a slight moment. Then I saw the baby. She was a dream, a lovely but scary dream.

I took thirty days' leave and it was delightful. I don't remember much about that time, except holding Michelle and drinking. We found an apartment and Sib and Michelle moved out of her parents' house. This was a big move to have our own place. It still all seemed like a dream. There were nights I became very restless when I could not drink as much as I wanted because I didn't want to upset Sib.

The thirty days were over and I returned to the ship. I found that the old World War II veteran, who had been busted from chief to petty officer third class, had hung himself in the storeroom. They said he was an alcoholic. I swallowed the information and didn't think about him again for almost a decade. The other news was great. I was getting out of the Navy in four months.

On October 18, 1968, all the papers had been signed which released me from active duty. I marched off the ship and saluted the Officer of the Day as I asked permission to go ashore. The permission was granted and I was off the *Higbee* for good. There was no one there waiting as I left the ship and I didn't give farewells to anyone. It seemed that I quickly isolated myself from everyone on that ship. Goodbyes were simply not necessary. I think I saw Dave M. on the way out and we just smiled for a moment and that was it. I swung my seabag over my shoulder and strode away from the ship. There were no feelings as I walked away, just the thought of what it was all about. It was as if I was watching a movie and I had nothing to say about what was happening. I walked away and I did not look back.

CHAPTER 6

Post-Vietnam

I went to work at a dry cleaners a few days after my separation from the Navy. My first Christmas home I worked two dry cleaning jobs so Sib and I could afford to buy some presents and a Christmas tree. I had a hard time understanding why Christmas was so important to her, but it was, so I did my best to get the money that was needed.

By January, two months after I got out of the Navy, I got a job at the probation department. It was something I had always wanted to do, to be a counselor in a juvenile institution. There were a number of people who helped to make this possible. One of the persons was Mr. Drake, the grandfather of a kid I had gone to high school with. He was the Director of Juvenile Hall and had told me to see him when I got out of the service, which I did. He counseled me to wait for an opening at a juvenile home where I might find my experience more rewarding. He guided me in the right direction and let me use him as a reference.

I remember getting my application to the county personnel office at the deadline day. It was 4:35 p.m. and the cutoff time was 4:30 p.m. The secretaries would not open the door as I frantically knocked. I was in tears as I searched for an unlocked door. Finally, I found one and I snuck into the building and was able to convince one of the clerks that, although she didn't have to accept my application, that she could allow me to drop the application on the desk. She was merciful and let me leave the application.

Out of about 60 applicants, I was one of about ten chosen as a group counselor at Orange County Juvenile Home. The county was building new facilities, so there was a large number of staff movement. I was thrilled that I had gotten this job and I thought all of my dreams had come true.

Then a feeling began to crawl under my skin and I began to wonder if I could do the job required. There was going to be some training. For that, I was grateful. The training was about three months long and it focused on group dynamics and self-awareness. A lot of role-playing was involved. On one occasion, we were given specific role descriptions to take home and told to return the next week and play these roles out. On the following weekend, I returned to the training session a little late. I walked in; an argument was in process between a woman counselor, Lupe, and a male counselor, Red. The debate was on whether the training session should be tape-recorded. The session dealt with our personal feelings and Red felt recording would be inappropriate. I jumped in and said, "What is important here is that we are all able to express our feelings freely." Lupe jumped at me and screamed, "You stay out of it because you don't believe in anything. All you're trying to do is look good in front of the trainers." It turned into a wild argument and what I had forgotten was that we were role-playing. I felt like my guts had been kicked to death, but I hung in there by mere threads. A few weeks later, I told the trainers what had happened and we all laughed. In a sense, I was embarrassed as I laughed, but at the same time I was able to see the humor in how hard I was trying to be the perfect counselor. Throughout my life, laughter had been a part of my person that seemed to help make life bearable. My mother seemed to have the ability to bring laughter with her wherever she went. I remember asking her, "Where you going, mama," and she would answer, "I'm going insane, do you want to come along?" Another time my dad was complaining about never getting desserts in his lunch for work, so my mom put an orange in his lunch pail. My dad didn't laugh when he first opened the pail under the orange tree. I held my laughter back until I saw him begin to smile. The next day we got apple turnovers. In the service when we were stranded at sea after getting hit by one of our ships, I began to act like I was a big time reporter for CBS and I interviewed some of the guys like they were going to play in the Superbowl between the U.S.A. and the Korean Communists. The act got laughs and it made life a little more relaxed during tense times.

While at juvenile home, I began to drink more during the week, yet I became very involved with the boys and their parents because I wanted to be the best counselor ever. I was complimented on my ability to run groups and be able to develop close relationships with the kids on my caseload. The persons responsible for our training and evaluation were three senior counselors; W.B., R.D. and P.C. W.B. was an absolute "space cadet," who had a tremendous insight into human behavior. He truly believed that one could see the "essence" of persons by the way they related to one another, particularly to their parents. He used the ability to express feelings as a measure of a boy's growth. If a boy could say, "I feel helpless, hurt, frustrated, angry, rejected and helpless," then, and only then, was he ready for release. These feelings had to be expressed to a peer whom the boy had developed a relationship with and to the parents. The counselor was supposed to be a role model for the residents, demonstrating the ability to express feelings and developing meaningful relationships.

During the first year, my focus was on learning what I thought made an effective counselor. My goal was to emulate R.D. and W.B. and help the residents and their parents. I had a drive to survive and excel; it was a natural roving energy that alerted me to the fact that politics were in play. I came to believe the needs of the residents could only be met if the needs of administration and supervision were addressed.

The philosophy of the program was based on the notion that kids could learn to relate to their parents and peers if given the opportunity. The opportunity did not surface much because there were so many wrecked kids who had been emotionally abused, and who many times knew they were not wanted. The residents were many times lacking trust in anyone, particularly their parents. Many times the parents were not really sure whether they wanted their children or not. They let their kids know this by ignoring them, trying to buy them off, driving them crazy with putdown statements, or double binds like, "Tell the truth but don't talk about Dad's drinking in the group." Foster homes were available, but it seemed the kids preferred to be with their rejecting parents than with foster parents.

I was assigned to work with an older group who ranged in age from 14 to 17. My first case was with a young man who had hair down to his shoulders, slightly built and very withdrawn. His eyes were dark brown and focused always on the ground. During our first encounter, he did not look at me. I asked him to look up, just for a few seconds, and when he did, I looked down with all the concentration and intensity he had been using. When I looked up, he had a slight grin on his lips. I said, "Look "Ese," you and I have to develop some kind of a relationship in order for you to get out of this place." I was trying to say, "Look, little brother, I know you're hurting and I know how it feels, so share it with me. Maybe we can work it out. You won't feel so bad about yourself." I put my hand out and we shook hands in the name of peace. We had made a connection and I could feel a ray of light run deep inside of me. This was the beginning of a career that was to become my life.

My next major encounter came in group counseling. The Sharks were my counseling group. I was to lead an encounter group with them three nights a week. My group trainer was J.B., who was very versatile and creative in his approach to group process. He was very much into focusing on feelings the kids had in the "here and now." Also, the group would chant, meditate, role-play and massage each other. J.B. was gone in less than a month because he was going to work at a new facility.

The group process was an experience that was truly enlightening, because in 90 minutes these young boys would share and touch each other in such a way, that many nights we would all walk out of these group meetings three feet off the ground. I really don't know, if after they left the

41

school, they changed their behavior significantly. But I know that the program at least stimulated caring for each other, and at least some of the tears, laughter and silent prayer that impinged on their lives during those moments were real. Many years later, I was to see some of these boys again. They said the program gave them some direction and real sense of belonging.

The other part of the job was keeping contraband (drugs) out of the facility; keeping boys from running away; and deterring physical violence. The standing rule was if there were fights, those involved would be returned to a completely locked facility. Fighting was almost nonexistent to the eye of the counselor. In other words, if there were fights, they were very well hidden.

Every two or three months, there was a major incident where someone found a "roach." When this occurred all of the 40 or 50 boys were called into a large room where a "town hall meeting" was going to be held. Uncle W.B., the senior counselor, would run these marathon meetings and the anxiety would soar for staff and residents alike. All furloughs were cancelled and all the doors were locked. The stress that resulted from these encounters was horrendous because it reminded all of us that the bottom line was keeping booze and dope out of the facility while keeping the kids in.

The stress traveled like gas and it manifested itself in our afterwork sessions we had at a bar or at Uncle W.B.'s house. During those meetings, rap focused on what approach was the most effective in helping the residents. In the middle of a heated debate, I thought, "Why can't we be honest with each other, why can't I be honest with these guys?" I felt a knot in my belly that tightened with the nausea of my absolute superficiality. However, the alcohol I would consume and absorb would help to untie that knot and usually everyone would leave and I would talk Uncle into drinking with me, or at least keeping me company while I drank into mild oblivion. During these sessions, I knew I had to return to work the next day. I could still gauge most of the time how much to drink so I could make it into work.

The next morning when I arrived at work, my body would feel as though I had been beaten with a baseball bat. The sensation was like being intermittently electrocuted; there were times I could not stop my body from shaking. I never questioned these painful bouts after my drinking episodes and I had learned not to question them in high school when I first noticed them. I would merely pray for them to pass, so I could drink more later. These mornings were the time I did individual counseling. I found it very difficult to hear what the boys were saying. As they talked to me, all I could do to keep from leaving was to chant to myself, "Oh God....oh God....oh God!"

I was not returning home after work and Sib was becoming very upset.

I was not calling and telling her what I was doing. On the day before Easter Sunday, she pleaded with me to return home after work, so we could paint the Easter eggs for our daugher, Michelle, and buy her an Easter basket. When I left home Saturday morning I had every intention of returning home right after work. I remember saying, "I'll make it, I know I'll make it, I will!"

That afternoon I really believed I was going home right after work. The shift was over and I was walking out of the front door on my way home and I felt good, almost content with life because I was heading home. "I have made it," I thought. A friend called to me, "Hey guy, how about a beer?" I answered, "No, I got to get to my pad." He cut in and said, "Ah, come on man, just one beer, what's one beer going to hurt?" My mind, heart and soul became scrambled, then the answer that came was, "One beer couldn't hurt anything!" All right!

I became excited and off we went to that dark little room where we drank beer. At two o'clock in the morning the bartender was asking us to go home. I woke up Easter morning staring at the base of the toilet at home, where I had vomited the night before. My wife was standing looking at me, with bewilderment and hate; asking me a question I had heard before - "Why?"

There was no answer to the question except to get up and pray. The pressure would go away. I looked for an Alpha Beta bag and finally found one that I rolled up and filled with paper grass. I took some eggs that had been boiled and painted, and hid them so 'Chelle could look for them. She was so beautiful in her Easter dress as she hunted for the eggs I had hid and I prayed the pain would pass, as I avoided Sib's eyes. Somehow the day began to pass and by noon I was drinking again. The following days were filled with work and booze, school and booze.

I was enrolled at Cal State Fullerton and it was a different experience than junior college because I had grown enough to sense the answer to passing a course was that the professors' values determined their exams. In other words, what seemed important to them, was what I found in the tests. I had an insatiable desire to graduate and to do well academically. I listened to the professors' biases and to the tone of their voices as they discussed various concepts and theories. The theory was always presented as a "coathanger" to "hang concepts." The test of the theory would be whether the hypotheses, so called intellectual guesses, that were derived from the theory held water. Theories that were productive produced bags that held water.

A theory that impressed me presented the idea that society was made up of strata or levels and circulation of the elite was inevitable. It was Pareto who said, "Great revolutions have been no more than the struggles of new elites to displace old ones, with the "people" serving as its humble soldiers." The latter probably believed they were fighting for what they called justice, liberty, humanity; and many of the leaders probably thought the same thing. However, the real goal was the establishment of the new elite.

The former was my observed reality. What had been accomplished as a result of Vietnam? Nothing. Not a Goddamn thing! My heart said, "Forget Vietnam, forget Vietnam." My heart was very heavy from hate and confusion. I continued to focus on passing the courses and becoming intensely involved with the notions presented in the various theories that attempted to describe, and predict, social behavior.

During this period, I cannot recollect any particularly inspiring professor, except for one. The last course I took before I graduated was taught by a man who was not like any other carrier of information and knowledge that I had ever met. His name was Sharma, and I walked into his classroom in 1970. It was the last semester of my undergraduate work. The course was titled, "Quest for Self, East and West" and it was out of my major area. I was very ill at ease when I walked into the classroom. Sharma was a short East Indian man who dressed in ethnic attire and spoke with an Indian/British accent. I'll never forget his first words, "I would like to welcome all of you to this living experience, and I would like to make a simple request. Please leave your biases about learning, wherever you may have gotten them, outside the door, so they will be readily available when you leave class. Open yourselves up, and we will grow together here. Of all the learning material used in this experience, you are the most important. Therefore, it is essential that you be here with us in body, spirit and mind. However, if the river of life should take you away during our meeting time, I would only ask that when you return, please share the experience you had while you were away from us. Also, there will be 15 books assigned to read and chanting will be a regular activity during our meetings." The course was enchanting and the paths available to one's life were presented in a functional, yet mystical way. The repeated lesson in this experience was that each mortal life was in a growing state and that within each body there was a force, energy, karma, that was struggling to evolve into a relationship of oneness with the Absolute Love, Light, Intelligence, in one word, God. He explained, "Karma is also called the law of the circle which decrees that whatever we do comes full circle to our doorstep for resolution."

It was during this time that I began to feel a tremendous inner conflict because my father was still very ill, and I did not want to see him. There was a feeling growing in me that was unsettling. I started group therapy as a result of my inner pain. This conflict was uncovered in a group marathon therapy session, that took place at the end of the semester. The therapist accused me of relating to him as a father figure. I rejected this, then after confrontation with the therapist, I realized he was partially right. This realization resulted in my talking about my hate for my dad. I suddenly began to scream that I hated my father, then I began to hit myself. The group members held me down. The therapist put his arms around me and very gently said, "It's OK to hate or feel anger. But you don't have to feel that way forever." he asked, "Do you love your father?" "Yes I love him," I responded, "and I hate that he had to get sick. That's what I really hate." I then cried in peace, it was cleansing and refreshing.

The morning after the marathon group, I went to see my pop with my family. Michelle was two years old and Sib was six or seven months pregnant. On the suggestion of a friend, I was taking my father out of the hospital to eat in the park. I was very excited and so happy to be with him. He wore a sport coat and gray work pants. He couldn't talk but he seemed to be able to understand what I said.

He had been out of the mental hospital for nearly two years. A Chicano tech had worked with him and convinced my brother and I that it would be better if he were in a convalescent hospital. The tech was a *vato* who had grown up in La Conga. On this Sunday, my father hobbled to a picnic table to eat the burritos we had prepared for him. He walked like Grandpa McCoy, Walter Brennan, hopping on one foot and swinging his arms. After he sat on the picnic bench, I put a bib on him. He tore the bib off, looked at me for a moment and said stoically, "No." I thought my heart had stopped. All of my memories of when he was invincible shot forth to that moment. The respect I felt for him was immeasurable. Later that day, I sat by his side as he stared into space and I told him, "Pop, I hate what has happened to you and there were times I hated you." Then I kissed his slightly unshaved cheek and whispered in his ear, "I love you, *te quiero papa, te quiero mucho.*" He looked at me, for a moment our eyes were glued, then he glanced away. I thought to myself with desperate and passionate hope, "Did he understand? Oh, God, I hope he did." He finished his food, then we took him back to the hospital.

I was awakened by the phone ringing at 6:30 a.m. the next morning. I thought, "Oh shit, they probably want me to go into work on my day off." The phone was in the kitchen so I had to get out of bed. "What a drag," I thought as I stumbled to the phone. I answered the phone with a "Yeah?", trying to sound more asleep than I really was. The person on the other end said, "Is this Mr. Estrada?" I replied that it was and asked her what she wanted. She informed me that my father had ceased breathing at 6:15 a.m. My throat felt so dry and I felt helpless. It was really true. I had imagined this so many times before. I thought I knew how I would react. I even hoped he would die sometimes, just to get it over. My father was dead and I didn't know what the hell to do. I was stuck. What could I say? Finally, I think I told the voice thank you in a semi-sad tone and hung up. I stood motionless for quite awhile.

I had been in this place of utter despair before. I hated this feeling. I was trying to act the way people would expect me to act. F...F...F...F...F... you. Who? Who could I blame but me? It was I who had abandoned him. I contacted the mortuary and then I was directed to a cemetery. I then went and spoke to a priest who asked if I was a Catholic. I screamed, "What the hell difference does it make?" He very calmly said, "No difference. Your father will receive a service. Is there anything else I can do for you?" I felt stupid and confused because I had jumped on this poor soul. I just mumbled "No" and walked away. After the funeral, I was very angry. The ceremony was short and the drinks so long. I drank, and in the valley of drunkenness, I cried for me and my father.

My brother Vic and I became much closer after my father's death. We had been alienated from each other for a few years. We rejected the hell out of each other. My brother was a very supportive person, but I did not communicate well with him. I had high emotional needs that he could not meet. I felt rejected and for some reason I felt envious of my brother. Yet he was like a father figure, because he took the time to recognize what I was doing and what my dreams were. It seemed like I was the closest to him when we were boozed up. I began to feel like I was slipping. It was like being on a side of a mountain and all there was to hold on to was very wet mud, and I could not hold on. I couldn't tell my brother or anyone because when I called out there was no sound.

After my father's death, an impending doom seemed to increase. Going to work was terrifying and I wasn't really aware of what was scaring me, but I would be scared to death and I was afraid to tell anybody. I was reading *Demian* by Herman Hesse and my life felt like Hesse's character, Sinclair, a person without clarity. I was alienated from country, family associations, society and from love. This book brought a sense of hope to me although I didn't understand why.

I was twenty-five years old and in the midst of a life that was beginning to suffocate me. There was very little air to be had. During this period, I was arrested for being drunk in public. I had been drinking most of the day. It was the first time I remember hiding booze. We went to a friend's house that night, where I drank as much scotch as I could get down without getting everyone's attention. On returning home, Sib later told me, I tried to take the baby out of the car for a ride, but she talked me out of it, thank God!

I have a hazy recollection of running from window to window of houses in my neighborhood. I had this crazy fantasy that there was a lovely lady waiting for me in one of those dimly lit houses. So I proceeded to look into windows and somewhere along this path I seem to have become psychotic. I remember beating my face with my fist until I was exhausted. Eventually, I invited myself into someone's house. They simply threw me out and called the police. I passed out on the sidewalk and the cops found me there and jailed me. I vividly remember running in the nude in a padded cell yelling, "*Viva la revolucion! Viva la revolucion!* " My attorney came and got me out of jail. I had been at his house earlier that evening. He was the husband of my high school drama teacher. For the first time in my life, I had to stop drinking. I was in shock. Absolute shock. I thought I was going to die, as the suffocation increased, and all the walls were closing.

I remember after being released that early morning that Sib appeared to be disgusted with me, yet there was still a little support. She didn't want me to lose my job. I was filled with fear and guilt that my employer would discover my arrest. If this happened, I knew they would fire me on the spot. On returning home from work that day, there were two cops waiting for me with a warrant for my arrest. They did not put handcuffs on me as they had on the previous night. Nevertheless, they put me in the back seat of the black and white and we were off to jail. As we arrived at the police station, another black and white arrived, with one of the kids I counseled at juvenile home. I ducked, and prayed that he hadn't seen me and that they wouldn't put us in the same cell. They didn't. What had occurred was the woman whose house I had walked into filed charges to prove to her boyfriend that she was not cheating on him. At any rate, my sister-in-law bailed me out a few hours after I was arrested. Sib had gone to her aunt's for a few days. Eventually, the woman's boyfriend believed her or my lawyer convinced him I was just a drunk. The charges were dropped.

CHAPTER 7

A Movement

To this day, I have no idea where the job announcement came from or how it got to our house, but it did. The announcement was for a counselor position at a university in the Northwest. I had no real idea what the nature of this job was, except that its purpose was to help Chicano students with their college education and personal problems.

I was flown to this distant and strange land for an interview. I had no idea where I had landed. It was in the middle of a wheatfield that had a landing strip. I remember having an eerie sense of isolation as I walked from that little plane that had brought me to this strange place. It was late evening when the plane landed and it was sprinkling. A tall Mexican man met me at this tiny airport. He was very excited and glad to see me. He came across very dominant and talked much more than he listened. I was to stay at his apartment. We went to a bar and had a few beers, then returned to his apartment. The interviews began early the next morning. The interview process consisted of meeting various people at the offices of the Dean of Student Affairs. Then it came time to meet the Chicano Studies Council, the people who had demonstrated, petitioned and screamed to get this position developed and opened at this campus.

This interview was to typify how my career was going to evolve. There were many questions asked. They culminated with three major questions: 1) Who are you?, 2) How do you choose to identify ethnically and politically?, and 3) How committed are you to the Chicano movement and the plight of the suffering Chicano people?

My answer to the first question was simple. "I am whoever I have to be to survive in this hypocritical, inconsistent, insensitive, hostile and righteously screwed-up world." I believe my verbal answer alluded to experiencing poverty, discrimination, prejudice and social rejection, and still being able to fight for "*La Raza.*" In short, I was a fighting survivor who wanted out of Orange County and wanted to help the Mexican people.

To question number 2, my answer was Mexican, because my father and mother were born in Mexico, and I had grown up working with men from Mexico. Thus, my soul was Mexican and my institutional education was American. I was confronted for identifying as a Mexican. I was very defensive when I was asked why I did not identify as a Chicano. I believe I said, "I am very aware of the inconsiderations, injustices and manipulations that this Anglo system has perpetuated on "our" people. But I have always thought of myself as a Mexican. I am ready to commit my time, energy, and my very life, if needed, to help Chicanos in the prisons, labor fields and here at the university." Down deep inside I wanted to cry and perhaps I did. I really don't remember. I know it was a very emotional moment because in my soul I was Chicano, a Mexican American that was discovering that the Americans of Mexican descent had a culture very distinct from the Mexican national. However, I had worked three years as a group counselor and had been a consultant to a community college Learning Skills and Counseling Center for nearly a year. I was able to expound on what I saw as a counseling program that would help Chicanos succeed at the university. I expressed that self-worth was the basis of motivation. It was important that Chicano students learn their culture and personal value. Because of this value, they could begin to use tutors and counseling as vehicles to more success. Moreover, that this success be shared with the Chicano community on campus and back home. It appeared that the committee was pleased with my answers, because three weeks later the job was mine.

I drove Sib, 'Chelle and our new infant Gabriel, to this new and somewhat foreign land that was to be our home. I was on the University staff as a counselor and instructor. The university was much like the Navy destroyer I had been on, except that the ranks of the officers were not as clear and the politics were at times nauseating. The nausea was from the obvious racism that permeated the attitude which some officials had about the opportunity that Chicanos were given to learn the skills needed to succeed.

This period of my life was extremely energetic. It was as if I had been waiting for this opportunity all of my life. I ran from class to class, meeting to meeting, student to student, prison to prison, jail to jail, and wherever I had to go, and as far or as long as needed, to assist a Chicano in need. It didn't matter what time of day or night; I would go. I felt like they were thirsty and I had the water. My image of the situation was as if I had been able to sneak into a grocery store and I could bring food to the rest of my family. In addition, I could share with them the formula on how to get groceries for themselves. The formula was in coming to believe that it was possible for Chicanos to not only learn two languages, two sets of values, customs and belief systems, but that Chicanos could also be leaders. This possibility would become a reality by nurturing the self-concept with positive feelings and thoughts about the Chicano culture and its roots.

The time was here for Chicano higher education to grow as never before. It was time for action that would result in more Chicano lawyers, doctors, teachers, etc.

There were many other Chicanos from all over the Southwest, who had somehow congregated at this university to educate themselves and then go on to teach others. There was one man in particular, a scholarly scientist who had come from the streets of East Los Angeles. I once heard him say, "I worship at the altar of genetics." This man was like the godfather or *Patrino*. He had been at this institution the longest, and he was a tenured professor who had led the battle for Chicano higher education in general, and specifically in the sciences. He was a strong, honest and committed man. Once in a closed Chicano studies meeting, I felt insulted by him because I thought he was talking down to me. I retorted in a very disrespectful way. We did not talk for some time. Some years later I was to see him in California and he said, "We had our differences, but now those times have passed," and we shook hands. It was a real honor to know him.

After my first year in the Northwest, I had guided the development of a Chicano radio show, a Chicano newspaper, helped to obtain release for two prison residents, and I was exhausted. I also had become addicted to marijuana; my consumption of alcohol had increased. I was falling apart and I didn't know it. I was purchasing a pound of grass at the beginning of each month and before the month ended, it was gone. I found myself in desperation crushing seeds, stems and powder, to have one more joint.

A year had passed and my children and Sib had become a blur to me. I knew that I felt very much for them, but whatever time I had free would be consumed by drink and smoke. Eventually, Sib began to disappear emotionally, physically and spiritually. Right before I saw the beginning of the end, I was in San Diego at a conference. I had been smoking and drinking all day. I went across the Mexican border and I began to act crazy and erratic. I started running through the streets of Tijuana like I was a Mexican merchant trying to sell "dignity" to the Anglo customers. I embarrassed Sib one more time. However, as a result of these antics, I was invited to speak at a small college in Colorado. There were a couple of guys from Colorado who saw what I was doing in my clowning, was spilling my hostility on the Anglos by insulting them. I was invited to go to Colorado and insult the Anglos over there.

I went to a university in Colorado and met their expectations. At a large conference in the campus auditorium, I proceeded to denounce the white educational process as insensitive and astutely manipulative. I invited the Director of Counseling up to the stage and asked him to bend over and I left him in that position for some time. I told him that was how one began to empathize with the problems of the Chicano people. The man looked up at me embarrassed and flushed. I didn't mean to hurt this person, but I felt the example had to be made. I felt guilty, momentarily, but I swallowed the feeling.

I then spoke of contemporary *"curanderismo"* and contemporary Chicano counseling approach based on belief, ritual and ceremony. I spoke of Chicano people learning that their strength was in the belief that there was hope in the world, that hope came from the historical reality that they had survived despite the horrendous sociopolitical atrocities that had been levied against them. Secondly, the ritual of *"locura"* (craziness) could be translated into productive energy that could redirect the *"envidia"* (jealousy) that had destroyed past efforts to unite. The ceremony was the love action for families, color, music, food and commitment to life until death. These thoughts were never fully developed on paper, but I believed there was therapeutic value in them for Chicano people.

During the Colorado visit, I was asked to stay two extra days and I did. I was scheduled to speak to a group of young boys at 3:00 p.m. I began to drink, smoke and swallow pills early that morning. By 3:00 p.m. I was bombed out of my mind and somehow I made it to the boys' gym. As I spoke, I left my body and I saw myself lying to these kids. I was telling them that there was a tremendous opportunity waiting for them, if they were willing to see and feel the cultural realities to accept our history and remember that we are Indian and Spanish, but the truth was our Indian fathers had been betrayed by a person who had given up on her people, "La Milinche." Then, the terror became overwhelming. A fear filled me that is beyond description. I ran out of the gym and down the street in a rage. The building and the people were slowly melting away. That didn't scare me. What scared me was the hollowness that was beginning to engulf my being. I was becoming acutely aware of a self-loathing that was beginning to take form. The insanity increased. I was walking and stumbling through the streets of this town in a state of paranoia, not really knowing what I feared. I would sprint, then slow down and look around, finding it difficult to see clearly. I tried knocking on doors but no one answered. I finally made it back to the place I was staying and I remember calling Sib, crying out for help. I don't remember what we talked about except that it must have helped because I was able to go to sleep. The next morning, I went to a Mexican fiesta and no one who had seen my display the day before made mention of it. I did not know what was real anymore.

A few months later, I was in California with Sib and the kids. In a drunken fit, I spat at Sib's face in front of her parents and relatives. All of her relatives looked at me in disgust. I felt like an animal who had rabies. I had lost control and I was unpredictable. On our return to the Northwest, she told me that something had snapped. Sib had lost respect for me and she was losing whatever feeling she had for me. There were numerous incidents where I had lost control of myself and had abused her emotionally. She was telling me that she was not sure of our marriage continuing.

By this time I had finished my master's degree in counseling. There had been many nights that I was totally inebriated and I don't know how I got home. That was not the frightening part of my life. The scary part was I didn't know what was wrong and my life was slipping out of my hands.

I was obsessed with doing something significant to help "my people." I remember Carl Rogers, the creator of client-centered therapy, was on campus for a conference on his theory. I walked into a large hall where he was standing surrounded by people. I walked over to him and handed him a letter. The letter said, "Please meet with me alone. I need to talk to you about Chicano issues in therapy." Somehow, we got some time alone and I began to attack his approach as ineffective for Chicano people. I remember building myself up into a rage as he nodded and said, "You seem angry." I said, "Yes, I'm angry," and I walked away empty and bewildered. "What the hell is happening to me?," I thought.

Time became very blurry around this period. There were a number of people who thought I was losing my mind and there was no one close to me. I was alone and the walls were closing in on me very rapidly. Then one morning, Sib woke me up. She was in tears and she begged me to leave her and the kids. She said something like, "You have to leave us, you're killing me, I can't stand it anymore." I had just a little pride left. I left immediately.

The separation probably was very instrumental in saving my life. Being apart from Sib and the children was very painful, but it forced me to look at my son, daughter and wife. I began to see the kids more than when I lived with them. I mean I saw their faces and heard the tone of their voices before I swallowed the booze and pills that kept me going.

My professional life had improved. I had become Assistant Dean of Students and a lecturer in the Department of Education at a new university not far from my family's home. However, I was absolutely internally warped. I could not accept the fact that Sib did not want me to return home. I pleaded and begged but she would not move. Finally, one night she screamed at me, "I don't want to be your woman." A short time later, she informed me that she was in love with another man who had been my closest friend over the last two years. I felt like she had taken a razor blade and cut my throat. I cried out, "You can't love him." She responded, "I do," and she began to cry as she left my office.

That same afternoon, a girl who was a student of mine came to my office to discuss a project. I knew she was married, and I knew she was mine if I wanted her. That night she came to my new apartment and we made love. A knock interrupted our lovemaking. I jumped to put my pants on and answer the door. Her husband was standing there, asking where she was. He said, "I thought she had come to a meeting here." I told him she had, but she had left with the students. He left and soon she was gone. I swore I wouldn't do that again, but I did. I wanted desperately to make my pain go, right now. I was obsessed with getting Sib back, but that part of my life became more complicated than ever. I tried to force her into taking me back. I threatened that if she didn't, I would divorce her. She was afraid I would take the kids away from her, but I wouldn't have. All I wanted was to return. She gave in to me and I returned home with much reservation.

I returned to the home I had purchased for her and the kids. In one week it happened. I came home one day and my daughter told me that her mother had gone somewhere with the man she had declared her love for. I went insane and stormed to the car to find her and the S.O.B. After driving in a rage, I found her car and I prayed he was with her. He wasn't, but she informed me that he was her friend and he would remain her friend, no matter what. I was confused, bizarrely confused. I wanted to kill her, kill him, kill me, kill, kill! I was powerless. I called a friend and the friend said, "Get the hell out of that house now!"

Shortly after the above incident, I talked to a psychiatrist, who had the respect of the university counseling faculty, about my plight. His comment was, "If you stay in that situation with your wife and her boyfriend, you might end up dead. At any rate, if I were in it, I certainly would consider killing myself." I didn't go back to see him.

I got the divorce. However, Sib and I continued to see each other. I could not let her go, or she me. I drank more, smoked more, swallowed more pills, finished my doctorate coursework, and had a very short affair with a respected female professor, who had been my dear friend. Nothing worked and I was becoming more exhausted and depressed. I wanted to die because everything I touched got rotten real quick.

I remember hearing that a friend of mine, a black guy who was an esteemed member of the university staff, had taken a gun and blown his brains out. I had spoken with this guy only a few days before and, in a way, envied his apparent confidence, social adequacy, and his professional status. Shortly after the news of his death, I was arrested for drunk driving. I refused to take the breathalyzer test and my license was revoked for six months. The officer that arrested me tried to give me a break by explaining the law to me, but I insisted on doing it my way and my way was definitely the wrong way. I went on a seventeen day binge and for the first time in my life, I was conscious that my body was craving alcohol. I took my son, who was now four years old, to Canada with me, and remember coming to at times and not knowing where he was. One morning he walked up to me and looked right through me and said, "Dad, you smell." I was dirty; it had been some time since I had taken a shower or brushed my teeth. My God, I thought, how I had felt when my dad used to come home from his weekend outings, beat up, soiled and dirty. God, I didn't want to hurt my son, and I didn't mean to hurt my daughter and my family. "God damn, son of a bitch." I had to have a drink. Later that day, I left my son in the car by himself, while I went into a beer bar to have that "one" drink. When I returned to the car, he was asleep. He looked so beautiful that tears wanted to flow, but it was as if my faucet had been rusted tight. I drove home hoping that I could stop the madness that seemed to grow in the pit of my stomach. Thinking that if only Sib and I could get back together everything would be okay. It was a lovely drive. The road was bordered by forest on both sides and I thought how perfect the forest looked from far away, then how that perfection disappeared when you were right in the middle of it.

I decided to stop at a friend's house about seventy miles from Gabe's home. The friend was a Coeur D'Alene Indian who was part Mexican. She was about fifty years old and I considered her a wise woman. I told her my problems while Gabe played outside with her kids. She said, "Why don't you call Sib right now and see if she will go out with you?" I called Sib and she already had a date. I was burning up inside at the rejection. I got Gabe home and prayed that I would not run into Sib and her date. She came to the door to welcome Gabe. I hugged him and quickly drove away trying not to look back.

After that experience with Gabe, I tried to stop drinking and I was successful for two weeks. During this period, I made a deal with myself. I would just smoke grass. I went on a vacation to Newport Beach, California and it had been almost two weeks since I had swallowed a drink of booze. I was making it on grass alone. I went to a party there and it was a very calm atmosphere. People were sipping wine out of tall crystal glasses that were only partially filled. I became very resentful because they were sipping and because I couldn't have any. Finally, I couldn't stand it anymore so I went into the kitchen and looked around to be sure that no one saw what I was about to do. The coast was clear, so I proceeded to pour me a large tumbler of this quality wine that they were all purring about and guzzled the tumbler down. Then, I filled a crystal glass and went back into the living room and sipped the wine just like them. However, something very strange happened, I didn't get loaded or feel anything. I was petrified with fear. Why didn't it work?

In the midst of my fear a light went on in my head, or perhaps my soul. A man had carried a message to me some time ago that there was a program that worked for alcoholics. All I remember him saying was, "It works, it works, let it work for you." He also said that I never had to be alone again. At the time this man talked to me, I thought he was just an odd and lonely man who lacked social skills. At any rate, I called the program that he had recommended, but it appeared no one could talk to me until 8:00 a.m. I was angry and I kept calling family into the early morning hours. I called my aunt and we had a conversation that startled me. I was attacking her for not helping my mom financially. I was complaining because we were poor. Then she said something to me that shook me. "Your parents lived where they did because they chose to use their money on drinking and entertainment, period." I knew it was the truth. I hung up the phone feeling hopeless and defeated.

CHAPTER 8

Spiritual Reality Through Mercy, Grace and Hope

What I'm attempting to share are the significant events, feelings and thoughts that surrounded what I call spiritual reality. As I mentioned earlier, Mercy, Grace and Hope were my neighbors when I was growing up in the barrio La Conga. Today, Mercy, Grace and Hope, the concepts, are my spiritual neighbors throughout a journey which is filled with a light that provides what is needed to move toward wholeness. The journey for me probably began when an inner voice hummed its gentle whispers, which ultimately grew into violent eruptions of terror, agony and slow, very slow, self-destruction.

When my dad died, I felt an intense pain that brought me to my knees, but only for a moment. I had projected my dad's death many times, but I never expected such an emotional blow. Alcohol then took that pain into the chambers of sedation. The important experience here was a momentary presence of "light." The light was a glimpse of peace that ran through me. However, the peace quickly disappeared and was replaced with self-loathing because of my perceived failure to love my father while he was alive.

A few months after my father's death, I was arrested for drunk in public, trespassing and malicious mischief. For the first time in my life, I was asked to stop drinking. I heard the attorney saying to me, "You cannot drink until we clear up this matter." I am sure many people had asked me to stop drinking before, but I simply did not hear their words because I was able to dodge what they were saying; or avoid the kind of people that would make those kinds of requests. Now I believed, if I drank I would end up in jail, lose my job with the probation department, and perhaps never again be able to counsel. Fear was my motivator. I stopped.

I stayed dry, without alcohol or other drugs, for three weeks. During this period I fasted, chanted and prayed. I read the autobiography of Gandhi and I thought about how he had struggled with his desires. Also, he had said that when one fasts, the fast is broken if one thinks about food or struggles with the desire. It had to be a total surrender. I fasted for two days and did not contemplate food. I was searching for the "way" to feel a sense of unity and perhaps prayer; fasting and meditation would help. However, after the charges were dropped, I returned to my prayer of choice, booze and beer.

The next major incident in my life that provided a moment of clarity was not my divorce, but a second arrest for drunk driving. At this juncture I began to question whether something was wrong. I had a constant sense of impending doom and self-disgust. The culmination was when the son told me I stank. After my son's confrontation, I began, for the first time in my life, to honestly try to control my drinking. The effort was fortified with more grass and pills. I remember walking through campus, with a lump in my throat and a knot in my stomach, looking at people and envying their apparent tranquility. I was dying and the end was getting closer. I felt like an animal in a cage pacing back and forth, back and forth, and my mind was focused on the misery that had become me. My prayer was, "God, let me die."

On one of these campus walks, a short, fat, little man came up to me and said, "I understand you have been asking questions about alcoholism." I responded, "Well yes, from an academic perspective, I have." He proceeded to tell me about *his* alcoholism, and what his life had been like when he drank, and how it had changed since he had joined a fellowship of men and women who helped each other to live and not drink.

Around this period, I had been invited to San Antonio, Texas to give a presentation at a college. I had prepared a presentation on economy, identity and motivation. For a short time, I began to feel like maybe things would get better. I stopped at Los Angeles on the way to Texas and went to visit a friend at Redondo Beach. We smoked dope and drank wine all day and night. Somehow, late that evening, I was walking the streets with a bum, sharing a bottle of wine and a joint. I remember a Jesus freak coming to us and saying we didn't have to suffer anymore, that we were forgiven if we accepted Christ as our savior. I laughed at his words and spit out, "Split, brother, I've been told by better." My memory took me to when I ran with the gang. I remembered a kid we had beat up, many years ago, and him looking up with his bloody face saying to me, "I pity you." His words ran through me like a cold steel blade. I thought, "Why did he pity me?"

I took my new friend, the street bum, Paul, to my friend Del's apartment and his wife reacted to Paul like she had seen Satan himself. Paul was literally shaking. I backed up a little and looked at him; his dirty, oily, filthy, shoulder-length hair, his hands caked with dirt and his fingernails long and black. My friend's wife, Sally, was white with anger and she was demanding that Paul leave her apartment. I said, "No sweat, we'll split, I'll see you both later." I left with Paul and I saw his desperation and his awaiting companion, death. The fear that grabbed me by the throat was the realization that I envied Paul because in a way he seemed to accept his place and I was struggling, trying to stay in the so-called normal world where I didn't really believe I belonged. As we walked along the sidewalk, we came upon a security guard who took out his gun and told us to get off his side of the street. I said, "You have to be kidding." He said, "Both you bums get the hell out of here." He was looking at me like Sally had been looking at Paul. Paul and I drank a small bottle of wine and smoked another joint. He disappeared into the dark to find a place to sleep and I returned to the apartment. Sally wasn't mad anymore in the morning. I apologized and she told me not to worry about it. We smoked a few joints and the time flew by as we listened to jazz; before I knew it, I was on my way to catch the plane for San Antonio.

I finally got to Texas and lectured on Organizational Development and worked diligently to help start a National Association of Chicanos in Higher Education. Then I returned home and after some months I had an offer to interview at Stanford University for Director of Admissions for the Masters of Business Administration Program. I went through a screening interview with a dean from Stanford University. He was impressed with my ideas and he had me flown to Stanford twice for longer and more intensive interviews. Shortly thereafter, I was offered a job at one of the University of California campuses and I accepted. I had completed my coursework for my doctorate and right before I left, Sib expressed a desire to try to put our marriage back together. I was shocked, delighted and confused. I thought, "Does she really care or is she just scared?" I didn't know what to believe. A girl I had been dating for a few months was going to come to California with me but the night before we were to leave, I got drunk and she decided not to come.

Prior to the Stanford interview, I believe I stopped drinking for two or three weeks and then I smoked grass and took pills for six months. Finally, on my return to California, I began my last drunk. I had promised myself I would not drink and drive. But early on my drive, the idea of drinking began to play itself repeatedly. Finally, I stopped and drank three or four beers. Then I was stopping every hour and drinking as much beer as I could. When I got to Portland, Oregon, there wasn't any more room for beer. I was very drunk as I checked into a hotel. The next morning I picked up a hitchhiker who said he was going to California. He had a guitar and we sang. For awhile, it was like old times. I was buzzing and the world was perfect and I could do no wrong.

I was on my way back home to California to start my new assignment at the university. Later that night, after the hitchhiker split, I walked into a Mexican restaurant where I proceeded to insult a young man who was of Mexican descent. I attacked him verbally and called him a traitor because he felt the Chicano movement was not the only way to help the Mexican people. He felt that belief in Christ was the answer. I was arrogant and cruel to him. He simply smiled and sidestepped my childish insults. On the way out of the restaurant, he ran after me and gave me a calendar. He very gently said, "I will pray for you my brother." I responded, "Get in line, there's a band of people praying for me; it doesn't work." I thought, "How many people said they would pray for me?" Then I remembered a hallucination I had experienced in a drugged stupor, at a moment when I was so drugged that I could hardly lift my head off the couch where I was lying. I had first felt a warmth or light close to me. I wanted to see what I felt but I couldn't lift my head up, then from my position I saw the light, the sandals, the feet and finally the body and the man. I could not see the face. The words I heard from this vision was, "Why are you doing this to yourself, my son?" My eyes were now two frozen tears, as I looked at the apparition, and whispered the words that seemed to be lodged at my throat, "I don't know." Then it was gone and the paranoia returned.

On the above return journey to California, I came to the next morning, after the restaurant incident, very close to Folsom prison and I had no idea how I had gotten there. I felt sick to my stomach and my mouth was dry and sticky. My skin felt like it was crawling. "Oh shit", I whimpered, "Why can't I die, why can't I die, I just want to die." I closed my eyes and from the apparent center of my being came the word "help." That was the last time I drank any alcohol. "Help" was the wave that I rode to the shores of life. That wave brought me to a phone where I called for help again, and a man came to my hotel room and asked me, "What is your problem?" I gave him twenty different problems that were killing me. He asked, "What is your number one problem?" I responded, "Number one is booze and drugs."

Booze and drugs were the number one problem because they tied my hands and feet together, and they blinded me so I could not deal with the conflicts, victories and confusions that were created by the way I perceived and responded to the world, i.e., family, employer, religion, etc. But there was so much I had done wrong, I thought. How could I stay sober? The things I had thought, said and done to people. My life was unforgivable.

At this point in time, I was introduced to the experience of "mercy".

MERCY

I began to realize mercy as never before in my life when I came to understand mercy means to be forgiven as a result of divine favor when guilt has been established beyond doubt. As a counselor and instructor, I have spent over fifteen years listening to people tell me their problems and particularly their inability to be merciful with themselves. I found that without mercy, there is guilt and guilt is not having faith or confidence in one's feelings, thoughts and actions. In one word, it is the child of fear. In sharing my story, I see how my life and the lives of over a thousand people that I have shared with over the past fifteen years as a professional counselor bring me to this belief: that people usually are in conflict because they are frustrated that they cannot control other people, or situations. In trying to control others, they try to form people into their image and many times after they accomplish this, they are dissatisfied and guilty. They are guilty because they hurt, abused and disrespected the individual rights of their victims. Such control to many people seems to mean "pleasure," happiness or some other form of relief. The person or situation to be controlled usually has something the "controller" wants or perceives as a need. That "something" may be a feeling such as warmth, admiration, or compassion, but the bottom line is that someone is not getting *it*, or at least not getting *it* the way they want *it*, so they "force" their will. At other times, the inability to go someplace or get away from someone is what frustrates the person. For example, a man is working as a probation officer in the city and he believes that if he were working in the country that life would be better, so off to the country he goes to find out later that he must take him along *with him*. "Things" can also elicit frustration because people believe that if they only had that house, car, suit, shoes or dress, everything would be okay.

For people like myself, who tend to fall into a pattern where a need for quick solutions dominates our lives, it appears that our lives are always laced with the feeling that we did not really belong, and soon we become preoccupied with the feelings and beliefs that foster guilt. The guilt turns into a desperate lunge toward life, in an effort to somehow think or do what has to be done in order to fit, or somehow be able to act as if we did fit. For some people food, alcohol, sex, people, pills and narcotics, separately or combined, seem to soothe that unbearable feeling of uneasiness and discomfort, anxiety or plain madness for awhile. Soon life becomes a crying infant, that has to be kept asleep or sedated at any price.

The life of the disease is varied, but the end appears to be similar in that it gets progressively more intense and painful. I wanted to be with my wife so that I could share with her in parenting and loving our children. Yet, I continually chose to spend my time with chemicals. I can remember when Sib would try and say, "I need you," "It's important, come home," "Please listen." Then, when she confronted me on not responding, I would become hurt, angry and sometimes enraged because she didn't understand how tough it was out there where I was trying to save the Raza. Eventually she simply learned not to share with me because it was futile, and slowly she lost respect for me. I tried to control her feelings and perceptions, but in the end she was done. I tried every trick I knew to persuade her that it would be different this time, but she had learned that when she gave me the choice between her, the family or chemicals, eventually I would choose chemicals.

My experience and observations bring me to the point that death did not come to me and others like me because of Mercy.

I thought very deeply that I was undeserving and a very low form of life because my wife, peers, and the world at large did not want me because they would *not* do what I wanted. I wanted acceptance and received rejection. When I was told by other alcoholics and recovered drug addicts that I was welcomed, then I received Mercy. It was a spiritual experience because I knew this was a real beginning. In the first year of sobriety, I was introduced to William James' writing. William James believed that there are a variety of religious experiences that man could have. Moreover, he challenged the use of mental stability as a criterion of social value. Stability was not my experience, it was only when the drugs were doing their best work that I felt stable. "There is," William James said, "a type of religious experience that is marked by shallow healthy-mindedness and that denies real anguish. In contrast, there is the religion of the 'sick soul'." Despite the revulsion that they inspire in the "healthy-minded", James argued that such persons recognize the existence of a wider scale of experience. He expressed, "They recognize evil and pass into a state of agony, but in the process may eventually conquer despair." As a result of my miserable existence, I worked harder to contribute to the people I was serving because I was experiencing that I really had a choice.

A dear man, Bill L., who I call my spiritual window presented me the following poem early in my sobriety which served as an inspiration. A poem by Aldous Huxley described my visions of choice:

> "The Choice is Always Ours"
> The choice is always ours, then, let me choose,
> the longest art, the hard Promethean way
> cherishingly to tend and feed and fan
> that inward fire, whose small precarious flame,
> kindled or quenched, creates
> the noble or the ignoble men we are,
> the worlds we live in our very fates,
> our bright or muddy star.

In the past, my muddy star was unbearable and almost devastating. However, today Mercy, even in the darkest hour, is the light that saves me. I believe that many alcoholics, drug addicts, overeaters and alienated persons suffer from the "ism" of a deformed perception based on an injured self that warps the perception. This warped perception alters reality and can produce severe stress that results in cravings and urges that cry out for satisfaction. After the urges are satisfied, the guilt returns because one more time stress was managed by a dependence on a drug or food. Forgiveness has come easier over the years as my life is more focused on doing, sharing and caring for others.

I have a meditation on Mercy I would like to share with you:

"A light draws me to the eternal "thou", to participate in that which is making forgiveness possible. I need to have a "star" whether it be bright or muddy. The shelter is the belief that God is love, light and life. This means that He, the harmony of opposites, is in me, as me, and is me. I have a home and in that home I can be accepted or accept, forgiven or forgive, despite what I have done, or despite what has been done to me. What has been done to me or another, must be walked through, not that the results will be eradicated, but that they may be transformed and energy pent up in them released. All of it must be accepted and eventually transformed. It can be transformed if it is brought to an "altar" as a sacrifice, wherever that altar may be."

Gibran said it another way, "For what is evil, but good tortured by its own hunger and thirst? Verily, when good is hungry it seeks food even in dark caves, and when it thirsts it drinks even of dead waters. You are good when you are one with yourself. Yet when you are not one with yourself, you are not evil. For a divided house is not a den of thieves, it is only a divided house. A ship without a rudder may wander aimlessly among perilous isles, yet sink not to the bottom." I did not sink to the bottom, but I believe I hit bottom and that mercy brought and continues to bring me up.

It is essential that I forgive myself so that I can continue to be able to receive the light that is so vital to a continued recovery, and so that I may share that light with others that are looking for a way. Once I forgive or am forgiven, I realize a gift has been bestowed. This gift is Grace! The magic word is action, and action is enabled as a result of a gift - Grace.

GRACE

The man who first introduced me to this new path of living said grace meant to receive unmerited divine assistance, which serves to rejuvenate and sanctify a person's life. The most relevant meaning to me is the way that it is used by the self-critical when others are faced with disaster and disgrace because of actions or misdoings. The implication in this meaning is that most have behaved similarily, but have been fortunate enough to escape the consequences. "There but for the grace of God, go I." I believe others, who suffer from the "ism", a way of life that is a revolving door of broken promises to others and most crucially to self. Each day is a holiday, when freedom begins to nod her head. I do not mean to insinuate a hand came out of the sky and saved me, but my point is that today I am aware that it was a gift that my life was spared and for that I am grateful.

Over the past nine years, I have seen hundreds of suffering and practicing alcoholics in hospitals, prisons, city governments, police departments, and neighbors who are drinking and using just the way I did but they cannot see that they are killing themselves. The key word is *see* because I know I could not really *see* what I was doing to myself. It is this ability to see that is the grace or the gift to top all gifts for alcoholics and self-destructive people. A wonderful book came out in 1984 by the late Chuck C. entitled *A New Pair of Glasses* and in this title is encased what happens to many recovering alcoholics; that is, they get a new pair of glasses that they can see through. However, it is the responsibility of the self-destructive person to keep those glasses clean and safe by learning to live one day at a time and keeping life as simple as possible. These last two principles are great, but they are real challenges for people who have a tendency to project outcomes and to be perfectionists. I would like to share a story I heard that exemplifies the need to keep life simple and not project.

There was a successful businessman who was late for a luncheon. He got to the cleaners to pick up his cleaning, but it wasn't ready. He became very angry because he was going to be late for an appointment. Finally, he got his cleaning and ran to his car. The traffic was moving very slowly. There on the corner of the street stood a friend he had not seen for some time. The friend looked despondent. He called to his friend and finally got his attention and waved him over to the car. He talked his friend into going for coffee. Over coffee the friend told him that he had a loaded gun and was on his way to shoot himself. Because of the encounter, the man with the gun chose to accept the helping hand of this man, who was frantic about being late for a luncheon. The miracle is that he would have missed his friend if he had been on time to his appointment. It appears that grace was truly received by both. One's life was spared and the other received a free lesson on not projecting outcomes out of one's control and the value of keeping life simple.

A few years ago, I was struggling in my career. I was not sure what I wanted to do as a professional in psychology. The university was becoming very stressful. I was doing what I could to survive in my position when I received a call informing me my mother was dying. Two or three doctors told me she was not going to live. I visited her every day for 21 days. On the 22nd day, my mom opened her eyes and spoke to me. Her words were, "How are you, son?" In this crisis, I was given the strength to sit by her side and experience the presence of a loving spirit embracing both my mother and me. I also had a clear sense of what I wanted to do professionally. I realized that my calling or goal was to work closely with people and to spend less time on organizational politics that appeared to be bureaucratic and self-serving. I resigned from my University position and went on to finish my Ph.D. in psychology with an emphasis on chemical dependence and stress management. At first, I was frightened by what my emotional projections were producing. It seemed impossible for me to finish a Ph.D. but my guides simply told me not to worry about what *might* happen tomorrow but to focus on *what could be done today.* Day by day, moment by moment, I began to see the light my brothers and sisters in this life were providing for me.

For me, Grace is many things, but first it is light. This light has provided the clarity I needed to see some of the patterns of my life. These patterns seem to lead always to the questions of why I am here on this earth and what is the purpose and reason for this life. Is it to experience pleasure as much as possible? Is it to be powerful and make right what I believe is wrong? Or is it to reflect the miracle that has permeated my being these last nine years? Today, and whenever I reflect over my life, my life is for the sole purpose of coming to know, love and serve the Spirit of Life, Light and Love that has manifested itself in the lives of so many people that reflect the loving aspects of an infinite power. However, I stray on a daily basis, but life loudly reminds me how to get back on the path searching, serving and sensing this eternal love of the Absolute. The miracle of daily sobriety makes my efforts possible.

The miracle is much more than the blinding light which burst in front of my eyes one day as I cried out in the darkness for help. It is more than the inexplicable "hearing" of the call, deep inside of this shell where my spirit dwells. The call sang, and sings, to go on, to go up and forward as, to reach up and go on to this path with no beginning, no middle, no end. As a dear friend, Mr. Chuck C., would say, "Life is for free and for fun, for we are infinite children, with an infinite father, on an infinite journey." I believe there is dynamic hope for all of us children who suffer from the "ism" of alcohol, food, drugs, and other compulsions. The above statement is the basis for dynamic hope.

HOPE

I believe hope is the energy that runs my spirit, and provides the energy for light to see and the strength to do. It is that part of my life that looks forward and beyond. Trust dwells in my hope, for I am a living miracle. The duality that was with me in the '60s and '70s surfaces today sporadically as a conscious separation from Self. Fromm expressed, "Man is within nature and yet transcends it by the fact of having self- awareness and choice; he

64

can solve this dilemma by going forward. Man has to experience himself as a stranger in the world, estranged from himself and from nature, in order to be able to become one again with himself, his fellow man and with nature." Hearing Eric Fromm speak at my college in the early '60s, I realized then alienation was, and had always been, tiptoeing and sometimes stomping around the perimeters of my being. In the past, the drugs and alcohol overcame the schism from the infinite Self.

Today, the realization that the split is a part of my human condition, gives me a willingness to move forward and help me to accept that detachment from my pains or problems is sometimes the best solution. Today, I am not waiting passively for a miracle. Rather, I am living like the miracle is here. This attitude does not require rash impatience nor passive waiting; it is one of dynamic hope. Another writer who has affected my approach to people and life is Victor Frankl.

In the writings of Frankl, he reported that there were Jews in the German concentration camps who knew they were going to die, yet they had a sense of dignity and hope. They were people who were living their values. They were finding meaning in their suffering as they performed deeds that gave them a purpose to go on.

Today, meaning for life comes from the belief that service is the ingredient that melts self-centeredness. Self-centeredness must be melted because it is the root of my self-destruction.

Today, I know that my recovery has come as a result of giving away the time, energy, patience and love that was given to me, and continues to be given each day. In simple terms, I must give this gift away if I am to keep it. The same inconsistencies continue that have probably always been with me, but today I am learning how to duck the waves and come up for air rather than taking them head on.

One of the great manifestations of this has been in the re-rooting of my relationship with Sib as a co-parent. It was essential for us to communicate and be able to share our feelings and thoughts on our kids. This was difficult at times, but we persisted in walking through those difficult times where in the last three years we have grown to love each other as friends and co-parents.

As I review my journal notes, I see, hear and feel my being searching, always searching for the "way" to where the call comes. At times, my reflections uncover the light within. There have been persons on the path that radiate this inner sense of direction. These men and women speak of loving, touching, feeling, smelling, being here now - now!

CHAPTER 9

Sobriety

Sobriety is sometimes referred to as a journey of uncovering, discovering and discarding. A dear friend, Father Barney, who has passed on to another sphere of existence said, "Sobriety is like a guy being at a ball game, sitting in a crowd, watching and then deciding to join in the game. When he gets his turn to bat and gets to first base, he has begun physical sobriety; second base is mental sobriety; third base is emotional; and home plate is moral sobriety. He runs those bases as a means to maintain this gift called sobriety." Sober means to be free and sobriety is to be knowledgeable about life so one can continue to play.

When I came back to the home of solution, after drinking and using other drugs, the first thing that was made clear to me was that my sobriety was dependent on my willingness to reach out to others. I was told to put my hand out to other alcoholics, particularly those who were just getting started on this path of sobriety. I felt uncomfortable doing this but it became easier as I saw that people were putting their hands out to me. I was told to be "in" rather than "on" the solution. This meant to get into action and help in whatever I could. Sometimes this would mean to wash cups, pick up ashtrays, set chairs up for a meeting or go to a jail or a hotel to help a person that wanted to get sober. In short, the foundation and key was one drunk sharing with another drunk.

A man who had one year of sobriety became my guide during the first ninety days. He told me there were two parts to beginning. First, to admit that I was totally and absolutely powerless over alcohol, and secondly, to admit my life was unmanageable. I was to spend two weeks on the first part. I began to see over those two weeks that if I drank, smoked, ate or injected any mood altering substance, I was unable to predict the consequences of my thoughts, feelings or behavior. In other words, I truly was powerless over alcohol and other drugs. The next two weeks were spent coming to understand that my life was like a roaring river that I was trying to control. The reality was, I could not manage the task. Another way of saying this was that my life was unmanageable, I was powerless over people, places and things.

The first ninety days of being clean and dry, I was like a live electrical wire, jumping around like a chicken with its head cut off. I went where I was told, shared when I was told to share, listened when told to listen, and did whatever had to be done so as to stay sober. At the same time, I was obsessed with getting Sib back. I would have nightmares regularly and I often dreamt of drinking or using again. The mornings were terrifying because I woke up scared, with Sib telling me NO! It won't work out for us. I didn't know whether to get up or stay in bed. It was as if a parole board, inside of my head, was waiting for me to wake up, so they could decide what to do with me. I sat there in front of them shaking, begging for mercy. The mercy would come because I would remember to put one foot in front of the other and get up, suit up and show up! Eventually, the fear would pass.

Things at work were very explosive. I was Director of the Counseling Center for special populations; i.e., Chicanos, blacks, Filipinos, etc., and as usual the administration had a very negative attitude about the program. When I accepted the job, one of the executives said, "You're walking into a black widow's web." Administration had already hired my assistant director when I got there and his first words to me were, "You better move and you better move right and fast, or your ass is out of here." To make a somewhat longer story short, I was able to go to work one day at a time and I began to deal and cope with the challenges before me. I was able to do this with the support of the newfound friends who were also staying sober one day at a time.

Around the ninety day mark, I was leaving for work when I suddenly looked around where I was. I was living near the beach with two other recovering alcoholics who had three and four years sobriety. I saw the color of the flowers, the lawn and the Pacific Ocean. I began to cry, "My God, I am sober and clean!" I was coming to believe that maybe it was possible for me not to have to choose to pick up the "magic bullet" whether for pleasure, celebration, communion or relief. In other words, I came to believe a Power greater than myself could restore me to sanity. The restoration was *not* taking that hammer (booze and other drugs) and beating my face and brain with it until I was unbalanced, and then allowing the wounds to heal and taking that hammer and doing it over again. I must note that the "magic bullet" is a Catch-22, because it allowed me to live with my thoughts, feelings and actions, but then it turned on me like a python slowly wrapping itself tightly around my neck. As I reflect, at first alcohol made life fun and bearable. It was a real treat to alter my consciousness at will. Then, it became a friend to be with who always understood. Finally, near the end, my friend had become my worst enemy because it was directly associated with the major hurts of my life, i.e., loss of family, health, and self respect. Time passed and I met a lady who was very lovely and she told me if I took one step toward a higher power, that higher power would take ten steps toward me. Now, I had flunked God, so I simply believed that *she* believed there was such a God. One night I was suffering from the obsession of wanting Sib to come to California with me, but all I saw was her with another man. I felt like my head was going to explode. Then I remembered that woman, so I called her and said, "I'm ready to take that step you talked about." "Dear Father, I offer myself to Thee. To do with me as Thou chooses. Please release me from the bondage of self so that I may better do Thy will. Take away my difficulties so that victory over them may bear witness to those of Thy Power, Thy Love and Thy Way of Life, Amen."

I had made a decision to turn my life and my will over to the care of this new God, that I was learning to love and trust. I knew that I had many mixed feelings and thoughts about God, but I had come to believe that this group of friends who were helping me were a manifestation of a loving, creative and universal love. This realization gave me hope that maybe I could get back with Sib and the kids.

I had been sober about six months and Sib was planning on coming to visit me. I had anticipations of rejoining the family. Prior to her visit I began to write an inventory of my past life. I took my life in decades to that present point. I looked for the negative and positive aspects of my actions and thoughts. I then reviewed this inventory with a man who had a month more sobriety that I did. He said I needed to search more and talk about the effect these things had on me, in terms of fear, jealousy, envy, etc. So I went back to the drawing board and looked at what I had felt. I then went north for a doctoral dissertation committee meeting and while I was there I shared my written inventory with a counselor. After I got through sharing with him he said, "You are very hard on yourself, but I can see you want to stay sober, my friend." We talked for awhile and I returned home and thought about what I had done. Had I fearlessly searched under and in the corners of my past and present? Had I looked at my whole life? I believed this was essential to my continued sobriety. I felt I had tried my best. I then went to the restroom and got down on my knees and clasped my hands together. I asked this Higher Power I was now calling Father to help me be willing to give up my character defects and to remove any blocks I might have that would deter this wish. I then quickly began to make a list of the persons I had harmed. I talked to people and tried to make amends wherever possible; in other cases I just wrote.

Sib did not come to visit until the year was nearly over. My greatest burden was being obsessed with having her back. She came to visit and told me a boyfriend had driven her and the kids to California. My heart and guts seemed to drop to the floor with jealousy as I heard her words. I don't remember too much more except that I tried desperately to cover up my feelings. I had been dating a girl and I just was glad I too had a "someone." Before Sib left, I thought I would make one last try. I asked her if she would remarry me and she said okay. A short time after that, she called me and told me she really cared for this other guy and that she wanted to be with him. I wanted relief now. I asked her to please let me be. I never wanted to run into oblivion so badly as that night. I must have talked to at least ten sober alcoholic men the next few days. I came to see that no matter what happened in my life, I could always reach out to a person or persons for help. The isolation continues to slowly dissolve. I was ashamed that Sib did not want me and that she had chosen someone else. This was a test of whether I would go to any lengths to stay sober. I did, and pray I will continue to do so.

I became involved with various women trying to fill a void. There were some very embarrassing, helpless and powerless moments. There were times I was having sex when I really didn't want to. I asked a woman to marry me on a compulsion, and I lied knowingly. Later I went back to these people and expressed my regrets for being in part responsible for their hurt. I wanted to get married again, thinking this would fix me. I was obsessed with this. Eventually, I ended up dating one lady and we moved in together. I must confess that deep down inside my wish was to be with my kids and Sib, but I had accepted as much as I could, that this was not possible.

One early morning, Sib called and wanted to try and get back together. The world went upside down again, but this time I did not run at her call. I called her back a few days later after receiving guidance from my fellows. She immediately told me that her problem had been resolved. I just laughed to myself. God, where was she? And where was I? I had broken up with my girlfriend a number of times, then I would return to her and ask her to marry me and then change my mind. This was becoming a pattern so I broke up with this young woman one last time, and I called Sib to see if she wanted me. Perhaps I knew that this was the end. She told me she was fine and her relationship with this man was continuing. I kept talking to other alcoholics. One day I became very frightened and lonely. I called my girlfriend because I had to pick up my suit. When I got there I began to cry and I asked her if I could return. She said yes. I had learned she was seeing another guy and I became afraid I would lose her too. I was so confused, and reluctant to follow the direction that had been given to me, to live with myself. I decided that if I got married it would make things better; so we were married in Las Vegas.

During the next year, which was my second year of sobriety, my son and daughter came to live with us. Their mother, Sib, had married the man she was dating. She got pregnant shortly after her marriage. I had begun to make amends to some of the people I had worked with and I was trying to share with alcoholics who wanted to stay sober. On one of these days, my brother Vic called me and told me he felt uncomfortable being with me since I had stopped drinking and using. He said he really didn't want to be around me. It hurt that my brother was choosing not to see me. After we talked, I began to cry because I felt so much love for him and I was grateful for the support he had given me most of my life. A few moments later I got a call from a "wet" drunk who wanted to stop drinking and off I went to talk to him as I had been talked to.

During the third year of sobriety, I was in the middle of finishing my Ph.D. in psychology and the pressure I felt was great. There were many arguments with my wife and it was suggested I stay in the relationship in spite of my desire to leave. In addition, my oldest brother Pete's illness of cirrhosis of the liver had progressed to the point of death. I'll never forget going to the hospital and holding his hand while he was in a coma. I kissed his cheek and said, "Pete, I love you and I am glad that you are my brother; I'm so sorry for the pain you went through, but I pray to God you know how proud I am of you because you tried the best you could." Then I walked away. Two days later I was at his funeral. My sisters Nellie and Vera and their daughters were there. Vic and my Aunt Lucy, along with other cousins and many of the people from his church, had come to remember my brother Pete. I was one of the pallbearers and as I approached the casket, I noticed the trees rustling, the sky was covered with gray clouds and then it was time to say our last words. My brother Vic went up to the casket and then as I walked up I saw two *vatos* standing there with their khakis and Pendletons buttoned up to the top. "*Los vatos locos*, the hip, the angry, and the searching," I thought. I came up to the casket and then went down on both knees, made the sign of the cross. I then felt like a tidal wave had crashed down on me and I began to cry from within until I burst out in a series of sobs, NO, NO, NO God, please no! Then I took a deep breath and I knew it was okay and that my brother's spirit was at peace, and so was mine.

CHAPTER 10

Spiritual Reality Reflections

These last ten years have been filled with crosses to bear, but also with flowers that have showered my soul with their enchanting fragrances. The flowers are the people who have come into my life to threaten, challenge, love and console me. I am sure that I have also played those parts in other persons' lives. The difference today is that I seek the light to see, so I may not have to hurt or mistreat another person when there is no need. Time and awareness of my immaturity has provided a basis for continued growth in the direction of self-esteem, self-worth and self-regard. This esteem, worth and regard for others has been another major force in my growth. As one prayer says, "Even though I may not be doing Thy will, the fact that I desire to, will please You."

To please the absolute Love, the Higher Power, my Heavenly Father has been my spiritual quest. There were times during these past years where I walked through sheer darkness. The first was the realization that I could not be with my children on a full-time basis. Although I had sobriety, the cards simply have not included the first marriage being restored. There was tremendous bitterness in my heart for some time because of this reality. Confusion seemed to be my daily state and I wanted relief now, but reality came as I came to *accept* the pain for what it was. The pain was there to let me know I really cared for the family and to know that I didn't have to use a drug to see me through the darkness.

Another dark period was when I was asked to withdraw my candidacy from an educational doctorate program in the northwest during my first year of sobriety. The committee was warranted in asking for my withdrawal, but the bits of hurt and shame lingered. But I thank God for that experience, because the meaning that ensued made it clear, once again, that the people who loved me were interested in me as a person rather than in my title. A friend and mentor, Father Dave, often comments in his seminars, "I perform a priest's job, but I am not a priest. I perform an accountant's function, but I am not an accountant. I perform a professor's duty, but I am not a professor. I am Dave, and that's good enough today." It was he who literally took me by the hand and said "Come with me, Chago (short for Santiago), you're going to get your Ph.D." I responded, "How, Dave?," and he laughed that magnificent laugh of his and sang out, "One day at a time, Chago, one day at a time!"

A third crisis was the second marriage ending in a divorce. I had not yet resolved the issue in the first marriage, so I had gotten married for a quick fix that turned into a quick divorce.

A fourth crisis was the call I received telling me that my mother was dying. A part of me wanted to run away, as I had when my father had become mentally ill, but a power within me led me to the hospital where my mother lay. Her mouth was bleeding profusely. I sat by her side and began to cry like a baby. I asked, "Mamacita, what do you want me to do? Please tell me." I began to choke on my own saliva. Finally, I caught my breath and went to the phone and called my friend and guide Lyn, who became a channel for God's direction. I quickly had my mother transferred out of that hospital. The doctors and nurses at the new hospital assured me she would not live much longer. I saw her every day for three weeks; she was in a coma. I came to experience the denial, anger, depression and finally the total acceptance of my mother's inevitable death. My brothers and sisters came from short and long distances, but eventually it was my mom and I who stayed alone in that room. As I mentioned earlier, there was a spirit that filled my entire being with a sense of infinite love, infinite joy and infinite peace. There were trials and tribulations that followed her slow recovery. There were times I wished she had died. These thoughts came as a result of frustration. Finally, she was ready to be released from the community hospital and I called over forty convalescent hospitals. No one wanted to accept my mom, because she was a total invalid as a result of her heart attack. The willingness to pray for patience helped me to find a convalescent hospital that would take her. My mom got better and I saw her regularly. She was one of my greatest teachers, and I respected her philosophy and her right to be the person she was. She always tried to show me that life was a spiritual gift.

Those were draining days when she began her slow recovery. She was never to walk again, but she was able to eat and her mind was clear as crystal. She changed after her heart attack; she seemed more at peace. She had one fairly healthy year, then the last three years my mom's health began to deteriorate. She lost her eyesight, until she was completely blind. I would come to see her and I would hold her little hands and a part of me wanted to put my head on her lap so she would pat my head but as I looked at what had happened to her body, I knew those days were gone. I knew she was important to my development and I knew she had hurt me deeply because of ignorance, but more than anything, I knew she had been there so many times when I needed her. I knew I would be there for her. My mom began to have to go into the community hospital more often. In the last year, she was being rushed into Emergency and the Intensive Care Unit about every six weeks. I had not made any efforts to publish this book, then suddenly I began to work on it again. As I reread the opening chapter of my story, I could see the time was here. It was as if I finished the book, I would be able to save her from that ring of fire I had dreamed she was in when I was a child. My mom was in trouble and she needed help. I went to her doctor and asked if she was going to get better. He said she would not improve and I could see my Mamacita was suffering. I asked the doctor what would happen if they didn't keep taking her back to the regular hospital. He said she would die. This was the most difficult decision that I had ever made in my life, since her last life or death crisis. I talked to my brother Vic and my sister Vera, who had helped manage the situation, and we all agreed it was time to let her go. My mom's body expired shortly after we made the decision.

The day of the wake I went to the mortuary to view her body and to be sure it had been prepared according to her wishes. There were a few things that had not been done, so I pointed them out to the attendant so they went to get the makeup man. I was left with the body by myself. I touched her hands and they were cold and I looked at her beautiful little face and noticed the fine features. I knew, oh God, I knew this body was the body that something greater had dwelled in. And more importantly, I believed that my mom was okay. I could feel that she was in a better place and a rush of warmth ran through my body.

I miss my mom. It's been three months since she died, but I am so grateful I had her for as long as I did. It seems that she and my pop are closer to me in a way that I can only describe by saying it feels like they're with me whenever I need them.

Paz, a Mexican thinker, once said of the Mexican people, "History, then, can clarify the origins of many of our phantasms, but it cannot dissipate them. We must confront them ourselves. Or, to put it another way: history helps us to understand certain traits of our character, provided we are capable of isolating and defining them beforehand. We are the only persons who can answer the questions asked us by reality and our own being."

My being shows me "spiritual reality" is Mercy, Grace and Hope. Mercy has been bestowed on me and others. I know how to forgive today. It's very simple. When a thought or action is hurting me or someone else, I admit it, and seek the light to see, and the strength to *do* something promptly, to change that. Grace is the ability to take action on the stress that sometimes can produce fear, envy, gluttony and resentments that could take away the greatest gift of all - my sobriety. For me to drink alcohol or use drugs again would be like resurrecting a part of me that wanted self-destruction. Hope is truly dynamic, because hope works right now. It is hope that allows me to be aware of the meaning of H.O.W. (Honesty, Openness and Willingness). It is these three principles that guide my life today.

Honesty with self is foremost in my continued sobriety. I struggle for progress in this area because it affects how I think, make decisions and feel about myself in relation to others. Relating to others has been, and still is, very difficult at times. Honest relationships with my daughter, my son, my wife and other persons who are close to me are paramount to my total health today. There are various people in the field of alcoholism who believe that the essence of alcoholism is the inability to relate. My drinking and sober life experiences substantiate this notion. There are times, even with strangers, that a form of alienation casts a dark cloud over me. Today, there is a belief that works in my life which shows me that if I put one foot in front of the other, the cloud seems to pass. The longer I choose to stay immobile, the longer the darkness becomes a part of my life. I know that my self-defeating behaviors have not been removed today, but I know that enough have been removed that I can experience peace, joy and comfort in my life most of the time.

The openness principle is a slow process, but it has provided great gifts. When my daughter was 15, she shared with me that she had feared me most of her life because of the drastic personality changes I had while drinking. Moreover, she was not sure that these unpredictable transformations had really gone away until the time when she was telling me this. I praise the Power that allowed me to be open enough to hear the meaning she was sharing with me and the Grace that gave her the courage to do so. My daughter started her freshman year last year (1985) at U.C. Berkeley and she included me in her decision making, but more importantly, we trust and love each other today. This has taken a willingness to risk and reach out on both of our parts.

My son Gabriel has chosen for the past nine years to spend half of each year with me. He is a strong, quiet, loving and considerate person who has the normal teenage traits. He and his sister have been my love teachers. Sib and I marvel at the ability that Gabe and Chelle have to love.

Five years ago, I met a person named Kim who became my best friend, student and two years ago my wife. It was necessary for me to go to individual therapy and couple therapy before I could begin to have the ability to trust and be open to the feelings of a woman. Kim has opened doors that had never been opened and today I look forward to learning how to build a relationship based on mutual respect and love.

Willingness is the key to my locked doors. To be human is to be of the spirit. It is my most nurturing thought at this moment. It is a real spirit that moves me to the position where the intensity and labor of my compulsions are neutralized enough to get me out of me and into others. By looking at others and into others, I see my life, light and love.

I have walked through the barrios of my life and I see, I hear, I feel, I act and I believe that hope is real and it can be the gateway to a loving life. So, my brothers and sisters, one last dream before I stop writing.

A Poem in a Dream

The winds were blowing hard and the howl could be heard for miles as she whirled through the bodies of the people who were preparing to cross the border to a better life. These people were of varied colors, tongues, sizes and manners - there was an anticipation of danger and the wind seemed to fan the fire of fear. Without notice, a small brownish-red skinned old man appeared and the fear subsided to a peace and calmness - not understood by the group.

The people began to experience a sense of coming together in one place and one time to see what had been created by the greatest Creator of all time.

They began to see a moving art; hear music that made them float and fly to heights unknown; see time - past, present and future - as one time in one infinite capsule. Yes, their entire being was at the threshold of truth.

They saw that knowledge was the source that drew reality to them but that love could draw them out of themselves and unite them with the reality of the one loved.

They felt as if each person's welfare was important and they began to regard their neighbor's welfare as their own. The music of love was placing them outside of themselves, and they began to dance an ecstatic dance that enlarged their being and actualized their human spiritual life.

The old man had a twinkle in his eye as he walked away into the horizon and left the people to grow and fulfill their hopes.

The End, or perhaps the Beginning.

Please remember Hesse's words:

"EVERY MAN (AND WOMAN) IS MORE THAN JUST HIMSELF. HE ALSO REPRESENTS THE UNIQUE, THE VERY SPECIAL AND ALWAYS SIGNIFICANT AND REMARKABLE POINT AT WHICH THE WORLD PHENOMENA INTERSECT, ONLY ONCE IN THIS WAY AND NEVER AGAIN. THAT IS WHY EVERY MAN'S STORY IS IMPOR-TANT, ETERNAL, SACRED. THAT IS WHY EVERY MAN, AS LONG AS HE LIVES, FULFILLS THE WILL OF NATURE, IS WONDROUS AND WORTHY OF EVERY CONSIDERATION. IN EACH INDIVID-

UAL THE SPIRIT HAS BECOME FLESH, IN EACH MAN THE CRE-
ATION SUFFERS, WITHIN EACH ONE A REDEEMER IS NAILED TO
THE CROSS."

APPENDIX 1
Background to S.R.T.

There are a number of major thoughts that have impacted my approach to the psychology of whole human growth. First, the so-called neopsychologists, who believe social cultural factors, conscious factors and interpersonal issues are important in how a person grows. These thinkers provided the field of psychology with hope. Dr. Karen Horney espoused this notion: "Man has the capacity as well as the desire to develop his potentialities and become a decent human being...I believe that man can change and go on changing as long as he lives." Second, the humanistic psychology group, who are sometimes referred to as the third force. Under this umbrella is the existential approach. Victor Frankl is a major proponent of the above view and he too has influenced my approach. His philosophy is that to live is to suffer and to survive is to find meaning in suffering. He believes that man lives by three dimensions: 1) the physical; 2) the mental; and 3) the spiritual. His psychotherapy not only recognizes man's spirit, but actually is derived from this precept and it is called logotherapy. Logo means spiritual, and beyond that, meaning. Spiritual is not attached to any religious belief but rather it is a transcended higher value and belief.

Another influence in my work is the writings of William Glasser. It was Glasser's reality therapy that I used the first three years of my counseling career. Glasser believed that people want to love and be loved. However, he saw people as learning to substitute an addictive substance or behavior to replace pain. He recommends that the person be taught to become aware of having a choice and to direct his thoughts and behavior in a direction that decreases self- defeatism.

In addition to the above, the writings of William James, Abraham Maslow, Thomas Merton, Gerald Herd, Mahatma Gandhi, Parmahansa Yogananda, and Herman Hesse have all stirred my search for feeding the inner spirit. The result of continued readings, conversations, and my life experiences have influenced what I call Spiritual Reality Therapy (SRT).

SRT is a talk, writing and behavior therapeutic approach, based on the belief that man is a physical, mental, social being and can realize spiritual consciousness. It is a counseling approach for cracking the denial and isolation - a life of hopelessness that can lead to despair and sometimes early death.

There are basically four major concepts to this approach: 1) self-esteem; 2) self-worth; 3) self-regard; and 4) self-transformation. A short definition of each term as I use the concepts will follow.

Self-esteem is purely an emotional phenomenon that produces a state of well-being, inner warmth, acceptance, serenity and a sense of joy. This state may come as a result of human emotional contact with another person, perceived recognition by a significant other, the giving of one's time, energy and resources. Usually it does not come when one makes it a goal, but rather can occur as a result of acting on values and beliefs that fulfill goals.

Self-worth is the recognition, application and validation of skills, knowledge, abilities and willingness to put these personal and professional resources to work. It is the sum total of what we have to offer our environment on a physical, mental, social and spiritual level. The greater the self-worth, the more important is the quality of one's contributions to one's work, family, community and interior life.

Self-regard is the behavior which clearly demonstrates that we care what happens to our bodies, minds, friends, family and community. It is a reality check on our self-esteem and self-worth. In other words, it is "walking like we talk." What I mean by this is if we feel good and are aware of our worth to ourselves and others, then we will produce behaviors that will not endanger our health, our environment, and our inner life. When we begin to live without self-regard we stop taking care to rest, eat nutritionally, exercise, share with others and protect our natural ecology.

Self–transformation is the maintenance of those changes which reinforce the dominant lifestyle that support self-esteem, self-worth and self-regard. It is the experiencing of life enhancement values and beliefs that enable the suffering, alienated, addicted and hopeless persons to transform the pain into active hope, healthy growth, and freedom through 'surrendering'.

HOW IT WORKS
Willingness
Becoming willing, regardless of where you are in your life, to try to begin to practice the following suggestions. Now that you have read my story and have a basic understanding of where Spiritual Reality Therapy is coming from, I want you to ask yourself whether you are willing to entertain the thought of writing *your* story. Begin by thinking of the chapters of your life. Identify the significant people, places and things in your life. You might divide your life into decades or by school periods, i.e., grade school, junior high, high school, etc. Next, make a decision to take some time, 30 minutes to an hour, to find a place where it is quiet, close your eyes and

tell yourself to relax with each breath that you take. Begin to tell yourself, more gently and more calmly as you proceed, that you are relaxing and resting, relaxing and resting. Visualize this calmness spreading from your eyes up to your eyebrows, slowly spreading over your head down your body to the tips of your toes, always relaxing more and being more calm. Now that you are relaxed, slowly trace the first ten years of your life or whatever length of time makes a chapter of your life. Look at the people, places and events that formed your life then. What were the feelings, thoughts and behaviors during that period? Do this for each chapter of your life.

Action

The next step is to begin to write each chapter. The important issue here is to *begin*. Some people make a number of commitments like an hour each week for each chapter until the chapter is done. Others write whole chapters at a time. The key is to *begin* writing and to finish each chapter one word, sentence or paragraph at a time. It helps to believe that this writing will benefit someone besides yourself. This writing is an effort to offer one's life to another person and of course to your own self-growth.

After each chapter is written, read it and give the chapter a title. There are some people who reflect on their lives, title and outline each chapter. Again, the important thing is to begin writing and to finish the story.

After the story is done, you can choose to share the story with someone that you trust or you can choose to review the story and reflect on those parts of your story that produce a sense of self- esteem, self-worth, self-regard and self-transformation.

In reviewing my story and self-esteem, I have a tremendous emotional sense of well-being just to have gotten out that story which was in me. For my ancestral history and cultural roots, I feel a sense of continuity and joy for having a background that I acknowledge today without shame or hostility. I can see now that there were many people who gave me loving attention such as my parents, brothers and sisters, aunt, uncle, nieces and nephews, teachers, coaches, and friends, both boys and girls. If I look closely, I *know* I was loved and that I made an effort to love, and in spite of my failures, there were many times I succeeded.

My **self-worth** is abundant as I see how hard I worked to learn to pick oranges, clean clothes, learn to read, to act in drama, play sports, be a student leader, relearn to read and write in college, learn to be a counselor and instructor, take and prepare for the countless tests that are required to obtain a doctorate, learn to be a parent, a husband, a lover, a therapist, learn about the business world, learning to cultivate a relationship with a spiritual teacher, learn spiritual exercises for the maintenance of an interior life and try to add to my community by sharing my knowledge skills on a voluntary basis.

Self-regard has been the most difficult to sustain because I have a tendency to surrender to urges and yearnings that motivate me to overeat the wrong food, overpleasurize, whether it be TV, the theater, lust, or simply overdo. Balance is the struggle for those of us who are driven by urges, cravings and unmanageable emotions that appear to endure forever, yet we know balance and harmony is possible through daily renewal. The upheavals are decreasing, because I am spending some time each month reviewing how I have lived the past thirty days and then I make adjustments to produce a better balance in my life. My goal is to do this review more often, but I know growth-change comes slow.

Self-transformation

When I begin to feel extremely unbalanced, I begin to take a daily inventory of how much sugar, caffeine and white flour I am consuming and whether I am exercising. Also, I review my moods by charting them and by writing the themes of my thoughts to see if there is a pattern. I make contracts with myself to improve my diet, attitude, and behavior and all of this helps to balance me. The most important factor in balancing is to change the things I can and to accept what I absolutely have no control over. I must say that I seek progress, not perfection, in my transformation.

One of my great teachers has been Mahatma Gandhi and his words serve as an inspiration to enter an active spiritual life. Gandhi said, "I have not the shadow of a doubt that any man or woman can achieve what I have, if he or she would make the same effort and cultivate the same hope and faith."

Another inspiration is Merton's writings, which say to me that transformation is possible. Merton expressed, "Buddhist and Christian monasticism start with or from the problem within man himself. Man does not see reality fully and really (Bud-Avidya)." He goes on to say, "Our experience of ourselves as absolutely autonomous individual egos - from this error comes all the rest - that is the source of all our problems." Merton is supporting a way of thinking that can produce an awareness of human spiritual unity in the truth - love.

There is a prayer I have heard in different forms and it addresses itself to transformation. The prayer goes something like this:

"Lord, I'm not sure were I'm going,
And I'm not sure what I'm gonna be,
But dear Lord, I'm sure of one thing,
I'm not what I used to be."

In summary, self-esteem is a sense of inner warmth that can produce an awareness of well-being. Self-worth is a thought that places a value on one's skills and knowledge that results in a sense of confidence, and self-regard is the ability to choose to respond to the health needs of one's body, community and spiritual dimension. Self-transformation is the result of a positive relationship between self-esteem, self-worth and self-regard.

The next part of the process is to write the vision that you have of the next chapter of your life. For example, my visionary chapter is 'Surrender of Fear'.

I see myself more open to Kim, Gabe and Michelle, so I can share enjoyment and my perception when it is needed. I see us continuing to hug and show each other that we love each other. I see our family being able to work through differences and sharing our perceptions openly. In short, I see myself accepting my humanity with its struggles and, one day at a time, surrendering my fears and victories to the Power that gave me the light to see my alcoholic disease and my self-centered obsession.

I see the next ten years devoted to learning how to conserve and direct my personal energy so that I can serve my fellow brothers and sisters in my family, community, country and parts of Mexico. I see myself learning to take three breaks throughout the day to center my thoughts through breathing deeply, focusing on one thought and visualizing scenes that produce peace and calmness. I see myself writing a book for counselors on the philosophy and techniques of S.R.T. I see the development and implementation of a Spiritual Reality Institute that would facilitate the exchange of ideas, programs and writings on the principles of love. I see myself free of caffeine, eating less toxic foods and learning to see more of the world through the eyes of the child that dwells within me. I see myself less materialistic. I see a stronger commitment and follow-through on the above visions than ever before. May we all grow in the Way, the Light and the Truth.

REFERENCES CITED

Alcoholics Anonymous, 1955, *Alcoholics Anonymous.* N.Y., Alcoholics Anonymous World Service, Inc.

C., Chuck, 1984, *A New Pair of Glasses.* New Look Publishing Co., Irvine, CA.

Duran, D.O. 1981, Logotherapy-A.A. Spanish Speaking retreat.

Evans, H.I. 1817, *Brewer's Dictionary of Phrase and Fable.* New York: Harper & Row, Publishers, 480-481

Frankl, V. 1959, *Man's Search for Meaning*, N.Y., Pocket Books

Fromm, E. 1966, *You Shall be as Gods*, Conn. Fawcett Publications, 71 and 121.

Gibran, K. 1978, *The Prophet*, N.Y. Alfred A. Knopf, 70-71.

Hesse, H. 1965, *Demian*, N.Y., Harper & Row.

Horney, K. 1942, *Self Analysis*, Norton, N.Y.

Hughes, S.H. 1958, *Consciousness and Society*, N.Y. Vintage Books.

Huxley, A. In Phillips, Howes & Nixon, 1977, *The Choice is Always Ours*, Illinois, Request Books.

James, W. 1902, *The Varieties of Religious Experience*, N.Y. Longsman Green.

Jennings, G. 1980, *Aztec*, N.Y. Avon Books.

Jung, C. 1965, *Memories, Dreams, Reflections*, N.Y. Vintage Books, 329.

Merton, Thomas. 1978, *The Monastic Journey*, N.Y. Image Books.

Paz, O. 1961, *The Labyrinth of Solitude*, N.Y., Grove Press, 73.